The Error World

Also by Simon Garfield

Expensive Habits: The Dark Side of the Music Industry
The End of Innocence: Britain in the Time of AIDS
The Wrestling
The Nation's Favourite: The True Adventures of Radio 1
Mauve
The Last Journey of William Huskisson
Our Hidden Lives
We Are at War
Private Battles

SIMON GARFIELD

The Error World

An Affair with Stamps

HOUGHTON MIFFLIN HARCOURT

Boston • *New York*

2009

For information about permission to reproduce selections from this book
write to Permissions, Houghton Mifflin Harcourt Publishing Company,
6277 Sea Harbor Drive, Orlando, Florida 32887-6777.

www.hmhbooks.com

First published in Great Britain in 2008 by Faber and Faber Ltd

Library of Congress Cataloging-in-Publication Data
Garfield, Simon.
The error world: an affair with stamps/Simon Garfield.—1st ed.
p. cm.
1. Garfield, Simon. 2. Stamp collectors—England—London—Biography.
3. Authors, English—20th century—Biography. 4. Journalists—England—
London—Biography. 5. Postage stamps—Errors—England—London. I. Title.
HE6207.G37A3 2008 769.56092—dc22 [B] 2008026086
ISBN 978-0-15-101396-8

Text set in Sabon

Printed in the United States of America

DOC 10 9 8 7 6 5 4 3 2 1

For Julian and Mandy

Contents

The Perfect Stamp

Little do wives know how much men spend on their hobbies. But my wife is about to find out.

It is almost one o'clock on 22 November 2006, a Wednesday. I'm standing just inside the door of my marriage guidance counsellor's house in north London. I have a stamp album under my arm and I am in all kinds of trouble – emotional, financial, philatelic – a situation I couldn't have imagined two years before.

My marriage is over, but the reasons are still unravelling.

We have drifted apart over the years. I have fallen in love and I'm having an affair. I have developed a passion for someone I loved when I was young, and for something I loved when I was a child. I am forty-seven, and I can't concentrate on anything for very long.

I have built up a stamp collection I can barely afford, and it has brought me to the brink of ruin. The affair and my stamps, the two secrets that have brought me here to a small room in the shadow of Alexandra Palace, are not unconnected, for both are quests for meaning, the classic mid-life dilemma. For my marriage guidance counsellor the affair is a commonplace: a lack of intimacy and honesty with my wife, a beautiful woman who has rejuvenated my days and made me feel attractive, hotel rooms. But the stamps are something unusual.

Collecting fills a hole in a life, and gives it a semblance of meaning. When men get together to talk about their passions, we don't just talk about what we love – our cars, our sports, our romantic yearnings – but also how much these desires have cost us, and what we have lost. We try to regain what we cannot. We talk about the one that got away – the prized possession – as if that would have made everything right.

Little do wives know: I first heard this phrase from Michael Sefi, the keeper of the Queen's stamps. Then there were similar observations from the head of an auction house and my stamp dealer. They often spun a web of secrets for their clients, something they called discretion. My philatelic icon, a man who had the heroic name Sir Gawaine Baillie, had built up a collection worth more than ten million pounds, but his wife thought it was worth £800,000.

In the past I have wondered whether my affair was a sort of hobby too, a diversion from reality, a club of extreme enthusiasm. We loved talking about our love, and would sometimes talk of nothing else, shutting out the world with our own code. We knew it wasn't harmless, and that devastating and far-reaching things would surely follow, but we considered ourselves above life itself.

I found it easier to talk about my affair than my stamps. I was actually proud of it, even in front of my wife. In my mid-forties I could still ignite passion in myself and in another; better, it was a passion I had never felt before. And anyone could understand these emotions, the stuff of books and films, and of a million lucky lives. But stamps? Used postage? Who could be passionate about that? And who could explain it?

I told my wife of my affair in a straightforward way, on a walk along the Kent coast one afternoon, and things moved swiftly from there. Within a week I was sleeping in my office, within a month in a rented flat. There is a practical way these things advance, a clinical order to offset the hurt and anger and tears. There is professional help to call upon. But an affair with stamps – stamps as a mistress, just as uncontrollable as the wildest edge of obsessive love – that might take half a lifetime to understand.

My wife still doesn't appreciate my stamps, but my marriage guidance counsellor, who I shall call Jenny, is making a good attempt. After our session this lunchtime I have an appointment at an auction house, not to buy but to sell, a meeting that will place a monetary value on my private hobby, which in turn will affect my immediate future and the level of extended mortgages and maintenance payments. Rather than leave my stamps in my car I have brought them in, and I am opening the cover for Jenny to examine.

She is bored out of her mind in less than thirty seconds. She doesn't even feign interest. I say, 'Look at this one, it lacks olive-green!' She says, 'I know they mean a lot to you.'

I don't collect ordinary stamps. I collect stamps with errors, with absent colours, with printing faults. It doesn't take long for my marriage guidance counsellor to make the connection between what I collect – stamps with bits missing – and my family history, which has been a life with people missing. I mention to her that Freud considered collecting as 'compensation for loss', and she nods. She doesn't understand the beauty of the stamps in my album, but she can see that selling them is a great loss, another imminent separation.

Six years before, stamps were nothing in my world. I gave them no more thought than other childhood things. But I have since found that stamps possess a force greater than their subtle charms suggest, and that no objects so public have permeated my life with such effect.

Stamps don't leave you. They are not like people. They are like grief, always there, first as wonders at the end of a post office queue, and in later life as a silent link to the past. Aesthetically they may bring me to tears. Socially they may embarrass me ('You collect *stamps*? *You*? *Who once followed The Clash on tour*?') And financially they have the power to bankrupt me.

Which is how I ended up in this doorway, the end of a £50 session, £40,000 worth of stamps in an album under my arm, barely able to look at my wife, an appointment at an auction house in ninety minutes, and aware as never before of how much of my life has been casually transformed by small and beautiful things that most people are more than happy just to stick on an envelope and send away.

* * *

In 1968 I had a crush on a girl who was frightened of the Post Office Tower. The girl, Melanie Kilim, aged ten, was the sister of my best friend, and even as an eight year old I understood this relationship to have the potential of something socially complicated. The crush passed, I don't think I even held her hand, and now I hardly see her. But my friendship with her brother endured, and we meet every week to talk of work and children. Forty years have passed, and our lives have changed a great deal. But one thing holds firm: his sister Melanie is still frightened of the Post Office Tower.

One evening in April 2005, when I had just turned forty-five, I called her up about it out of the blue. 'Hi Melanie, this is Gus.' Gus was my school nickname. 'It's been quite a while, but I want to ask you about something I've always wondered about . . .' Melanie was forthcoming. She said her phobia began not long after the building went up in 1965, transforming and modernising the London skyline. She thought her fear of it might have something to do with the Daleks in *Dr Who*, and with the memory of a man in a neck-brace she once saw in the local greengrocer's in Golders Green. I was looking for a more obvious explanation – something sexual perhaps – but she dismissed this. She wasn't nervous of any other tall buildings, just what she called this 'grey-green monster', and she explained that what she really didn't like was the possibility that the tower might suddenly jump out at her. She would turn a corner in Soho or Bloomsbury, and there it would be: 'I think it might attack and strangle me – something to do with the neck again.'

To avoid this fearsome eventuality, Melanie Kilim told me that she had developed an extraordinary sense of positioning and direction. She said there was no street in the tower's vicinity where she didn't know what she would see when she turned the corner. If this was to be the tower, she knew the perfect diversion. She told me that once, when visiting the Middlesex Hospital, only a few yards from the tower, she had worn a blindfold to avoid an otherwise inevitable sighting.

The object that had always repelled Melanie had always attracted me. As a boy, I was fascinated with it. It was new. It was statistically engaging. Out of the then generally flat London landscape, it rose astonishingly to 619 feet – the highest structure in London, nearly twice the height of the dome of St Paul's. It weighed 13,000 tons and contained 780 tons of steel. The two lifts travelled at 1,000 feet a minute, and if you took one of them to the top you'd be at the revolving restaurant which turned two and a half times every hour, which meant you didn't have to wait too long to see my house in Hampstead Garden Suburb.

Shortly after it opened, the Post Office Tower could handle

100,000 telephone calls simultaneously. It boosted radio and television signals, bouncing the waves over the new London high-rises on to the Home County hills. The one thing it didn't seem to have much to do with was the post office. You could see the main letter-sorting office at Mount Pleasant from the top, but that was about it. I visited with my father in the first few months, and I treasured the translucent green plastic model he bought me at the gift shop, which I still have in a cupboard next to a toy grouping of the Chimpanzees' Tea Party from London Zoo.

For me, the opening of the tower marked not only the completion of a landmark, but the birth of something equally special – a commemorative postage stamp with a fabulous error on it. I first became aware of this in 1968, when a stamp magazine carried the news of this discovery with great excitement. There were about 55,500,000 of the normal stamps sold, but only about thirty with the mistake on it. I looked at a photo of the stamp with the flaw – a printing glitch: it was captioned '1965 Post Office Tower, olive-green omitted'. To an eight year old, this was unbelievable. The only thing that was supposed to have been printed in olive-green was the Post Office Tower itself; the surrounding buildings were all there, but in place of the tower there was only white space. At the age of eight I thought, 'This would be the perfect stamp for Melanie.'

I'd like to think that every schoolboy collected stamps in those days, although I'm sure that even in 1968 it was a hobby that was falling away. But for me it was ideal. I was part of a middle-class family in a middle-class place, and I lived in a comfortable house among neighbours who kept pets and had an aversion to noise after 7.30 p.m. Hampstead Garden Suburb was established by Dame Henrietta Barnett in 1907 with the aim of making 'a bit of God's earth beautiful for generations ahead'. About thirteen thousand live there now, and in recent years it has become a rural-ish idyll for celebrity television presenters Jonathan Ross, Vanessa Feltz and Richard and Judy. But the famous have always valued its seclusion: the dour actor Alastair Sim lived up the road; the newsreader Robert Dougall lived a few doors away. Elizabeth Taylor was born three houses from mine and remembers a perfect childhood: 'My brother and I would run through the woods and feel quite safe,' she wrote of her memories of the 1930s. 'I wonder whether the Suburb is like that now.' It was when I was there in the 1960s.

My father fitted right in. He was a successful solicitor in the City, he played golf at weekends, bought a sports car in middle age, took me sometimes to synagogue on Saturday morning, and wished me to do better in school. My brother, Jonathan, was almost five years older than me, effortlessly skilled at maths and the sciences, fast enough as a bowler to practise with junior teams at Lord's. I once broke his arm wrestling on the carpet, but usually (both before this event and after) we had little to do with each other. My mother looked after us all, occasionally helping in local old-people's homes, and entertaining friends with her cooking and charm. This life was all I knew, and it seemed ideal. I remember walking back from school with a fellow pupil called Will Self, who had still to discover drugs or novel writing, and learning that he was about to go on holiday to the Seychelles. I had no idea what or where that was. I hadn't yet experienced abroad; my parents went on foreign trips together, leaving my brother and me in the formidable charge of a Mrs Woolf, who made something called milk pudding for dessert every evening and wouldn't let us drink water with our meals because it filled us up. The most daring thing I did was have my hair cut by a man in flares called Paul whose salon was called Unisex, a word the entire neighbourhood found exceptionally unsettling. Stamp collecting, that most quiet and respectful of pastimes, was something that all of my neighbours and parents' friends would have approved of; it offered no evidence of nonconformity or the budding turmoil of sex. The postage stamp is a silent thing, and an emblem of social order rather than its opposite. I first became interested in stamps at the age of six, and by the time I was eight they had me in their grip. Most children grow out of it. I only thought I had.

When I was a boy I collected every stamp I could find, but it didn't take me long to realise how fruitless this was. It was like trying to visit every page on the Internet. After a while I began to specialise. I first narrowed it down to Great Britain. Then Queen Elizabeth II. And then Great Britain $QE2$ errors. Not that I could actually afford any errors, for these were the rarest and most expensive stamps of all. But I became unusually interested in them. When I was younger I could reel off a list of the most famous errors better than I could recite 'The Charge of the Light Brigade'. For example:

– The 1961 $2^{1}/_{2}$d Post Office Savings stamp missing black and the 3d of the same set missing orange-brown
– The 1961 European Postal Conference 2d missing orange and the 10d missing pale green
– The 1962 National Productivity Year 3d and 1s 3d, both missing light blue (the Queen's head)
– The 6d Paris Postal Conference Centenary missing green
– The 3d 1963 Red Cross Centenary Congress missing red

Well over half of all issues before decimalisation in 1971 had something glaringly wrong with them. There were huge white areas where things should have been but weren't. Icons

8

that the stamps commemorated, such as the Red Cross, were absent, thus making a mockery of the event. Even a schoolboy couldn't make many mistakes with stamps like these, and even a person with no interest in stamps could see the appeal. Tens of millions printed and sold, but on a very few examples the printing machine had run out of ink, or a paper fold had caused the colour to be printed on the gummed side. Accordingly, stamps with errors will always be more sought after, and dramatically more expensive, than stamps that are perfect. This feature alone makes stamp collecting an exceptional and perverse hobby. No one wants a Picasso with missing bistre. A misshapen Ming vase? A 1930s Mercedes without headlights? There are some coins with errors, and some rare vinyl records with misprints on the labels, but they do not form the cornerstone of a collecting hobby, and they do not make men bankrupt.

I don't think I mentioned the Post Office Tower error to my father in 1968. It cost several pounds. Several pounds for a stamp! You could send an elephant first class for that. My father would have been intrigued by the idea that imperfection equalled added value but he would also have doubted it (a chipped glass or an unreliable wristwatch were just things to be endured until you could afford something better). How was he to know that there would never be more than thirty of these stamps? How could he have known that a stamp worth three pence at the post office counter, and a few pounds from a dealer in 1968, would be sold at auction in 2007 for £2,100?

The first big error appeared on a stamp in 1852, an engraving glitch that caused the word 'Petimus' (trans.: 'We give and ask in return') on the British Guiana one cent and four cent to be issued as 'Patimus' ('We suffer in return') – and ever since they have been among the most sought-after items. Or unavailable, and tantalisingly so. Studying these rare stamps in my school-days I learnt a bit about history, particularly my country's fondness for immortalising events where grey men met in huge halls, and I learnt a bit about colour. I knew what bistre was, and agate, and could distinguish new blue from dull blue. But what I really learnt about was inflation. The 1966 Technology 6d issue, for example, which should have contained three Mini cars and a Jaguar, but instead had only the Jaguar against a bright orange background, was on sale in 1967 at the Globe Stamp Co. in William IV Street, just off the Strand, for £95. A year later it was £130. At that point the precise quantities of the error stamp were unknown, but today it is thought there are just eighteen mint copies. In an auction in March 2005 a collector bought one for £6,110.

Of course, I would have loved to have owned this stamp, just as I would have loved all the others. But my favourite was five years older. In 1961, the Seventh Commonwealth Parliamentary Conference was held in Westminster. There were two stamps issued. The 6d value was a horizontal rectan-gle with a purple background and gold overlay of the roof-beams of Westminster Hall, and then there was the 1s 3d vertical stamp. This had a racing-green background, and was split into two halves: on the top was a picture of the Queen printed in dull blue, and beneath it was an engraving of the Palace of Westminster and a mace and sceptre. On the error, there was no Queen. Simple: a white box on a green stamp. In the late 1960s, when I first became aware of it, it was the most beautiful small object I had ever seen, and remains so for me today.

Then, for about twenty years, I forgot about stamps. Or

rather, I neglected to collect them. First came exams and university, then work, then marriage and children, a mortgage. But when I was in my early forties, my interest ignited again. I can't pinpoint the cause – perhaps it was an article in the newspapers or a browse online – but my enthusiasm returned and with it just enough disposable cash to pursue the stamps I could never afford in my childhood. Within a few weeks I was visiting dealers and buying magazines, fantasising. I wanted the same thing now as then – stamps with errors on them. I still dreamed of being that London schoolboy who, in 1965, wandered into a post office for the new set of stamps marking the centenary of the International Telecommunication Union, saw that the 1s 6d value was missing pink, and bought as many as he could afford, which was twenty mint copies. I knew that would never happen to me. But maybe now I could buy that error from the dealer he sold them to.

It took me a while to tell anyone of my revived passion. I could only admit it to people I could really trust, people who would not think any less of me. My children thought stamp collecting both strange and perverse, and inevitably used that same phrase they employ to describe anyone over twenty-five in trainers and into rap music: 'Sad.' My wife tolerated my obsession but seldom expressed interest. Her questions were invariably focused on one thing. I wanted her to say, 'Tell me about the history, the beauty, the rarity! Tell me about *that* one!' but mostly she said, 'How much was it?'

My answer was usually the same. 'Not much, really.' But of course it was a lot – the equivalent of a weekend away, or a beautiful painting, or a year's theatre tickets. And the one thought I always had during these exchanges was, 'If only I'd bought it when I was a boy.'

I still have my first stamp album, with about three hundred stamps amassed between 1966 and the start of 1973. From 1973 there was a gap of one year before I started collecting again in a new album. What caused the gap, and what happened in 1973? I came of age, and my father died. And I made a very bad investment.

Gutter Pairs

To give up collecting at the beginning of 1973, if only for a while, was not a good idea, for one reason: bar-mitzvah presents. Along with a ridiculous number of suitcases and many copies of *Who's Who in the Old Testament* and *The Joy of Yiddish* (these are real titles, and very popular choices for people who don't buy many books, like *Schott's Almanac* today), I received a fair bit of money from people who knew I couldn't possibly want another suitcase or book. I should have spent it on stamps, but I didn't. Stamps were good value in 1973, but of course they always appear good value looking back. I counted up the cheques on the morning after my party at the Esso Motor Hotel near Watford, and I had about £1,200. Some of this went on Premium Bonds, and the rest went in the bank. I think I was allowed one special gift, something I wouldn't normally receive because it wasn't considered practical or informative. This is likely to have been the Peter Bonetti goalkeeping ensemble.

With £1,200 I could have bought a couple of fine errors, perhaps a block of the 1966 Technology issue with missing Jaguars. People who knew about stamps would have placed an order with their dealer straight away. For example, when the collector Thomas Keay Tapling was at school in the mid-1870s, an indulgent family member gave him £500 for Christmas, this at a time when £500 could secure a very fine house. But he didn't buy a fine house, he bought fine stamps. He received advice from one of London's leading philatelists, and the stamps formed the cornerstone of the brilliant collection that now resides at the British Library. A few months before he had received the £500 he had turned down the purchase of a rare Canadian stamp for $10, judging it too expensive, and he would never forget the lesson: buy when you can, or forever regret it.

By 1973 I had taken my father's advice: £60 for a stamp with an error was an awful lot to pay, and how could I be sure it would appreciate? That doubt, of course, was an error in itself. But a big word in my family at this time – and I imagine many families where the parents met during the age of austerity – was 'fritter'. The key to spending money wisely was to buy something that would be useful and last, something with assured value. Stamps did not fall into this category.

I didn't object to this wisdom; I embraced it. I received a school prize in 1973, the only one I ever won, and the prize was a book token to spend at the High Hill Bookshop in Hampstead (killed by Waterstones; now a Gap). I could have spent it on things I was actually interested in – the *Morecambe and Wise Jokebook*, a Sherlock Holmes – but that would have been frittering. I chose a hardback called *The Jews in the Roman World*, which I have yet to open, let alone read. It was presented to me on speech day by the mountaineer Chris Bonnington, an old boy, and as he shook my hand and handed me the book he looked at me inquisitively.

My father died eight months after my bar mitzvah and five months after my school prize. He had suffered a small heart attack some years before, and was going along nicely with a new exercise regime and a changed diet. The strangest ingredient of this was his special salt, which came in a tall blue-and-white plastic bottle and was apparently low in cholesterol. He took this with him everywhere, partly because he liked salt with everything, and would even put it on his peanut butter lest SunPat had forgotten, and also because it became a talisman. Have salt, will survive.

We didn't have much processed food then. My mother enjoyed preparing dinner parties, and she was good at it. Her guides were Graham Kerr (the dishy 'Galloping Gourmet' who used to drink as he cooked long before Keith Floyd got the knack), and Robert Carrier's *Great Dishes of the World*. These recipes specialised in aspic and cholesterol, and my mother was in her element in the decade of quiche Lorraine, tournedos Rossini and zabaglione. If any food could be put inside another food – beef Wellington, salmon en croûte – then it became doubly desirable. But there was a limit to her adventurousness; she never much liked the scent of garlic that was wafting through other London homes, and the chancer from the north who came round on his bike with shallots and garlic around his neck soon learnt not to bother at our house. The only commercial tradesmen my mother welcomed were the knife sharpener and the delivery boy from a shop called Panzer's, which specialised not in tanks, but in goodness from the old country – marzipan, pickles, stock cubes, sausages, sauerkraut. We were long past the age of austerity and Marguerite Patten's mock desserts, but she still ran a cautious kitchen. She kept leftovers until it was no longer possible to remember the original meal from which they derived, and she peeled and boiled everything until it hung by its last fibre; one more scalding minute in those pans, and her carrots would have just been orange water. My mother's signature dishes were usually things that rolled: beef olives, matzo balls and rum babas. But we all judged every meal delicious, and only once can I remember acute drama and hunger and tears, the day our lazy basset hound Gus – who had never leapt up to anything in his life – leapt up to steal an entire cooling leg of lamb.

But fake salt came from a different kitchen, the encroaching world of edible chemicals. As the 1970s drew on, everything that could be made false, was. Pleather, fake fur, the wood-finish around our television – all sold not as a replacement but an improvement. This all sat comfortably with my father's false back teeth and the soft top on his 1971 Triumph Vitesse, his mid-life-crisis car. He bought this just before his real mid-life crisis, something awful and mysterious that happened at the office one day and hung over him and our family for months. In fact, he may never have recovered from it.

My father was a solicitor at one of the oldest and most Jewish city firms: Herbert Oppenheimer, Nathan & Vandyk. My grandfather Leopold had paid for him to be taken on by Harry Louis Nathan (later Lord Nathan) in 1936, and his Articles of Clerkship reveal his true name: Herbert Sidney Garfunkel. He was born in Hamburg in 1919, and moved to England at Easter 1934. His parents, of banking stock, remained in Germany until 1939, but there was no mistaking the direction of the country after Hitler's ascendancy in 1933. (My mother, born in Wesermunde in 1925, also left Germany in 1934, moving with her parents and sister to Jerusalem.)

My father became a pupil at the Perse School, Cambridge, excelling at most things apart from sport. He was a lance-corporal in the Officer Training Corps, and held the same post when he joined the Durham Light Infantry in 1940. Towards the end of the war he was working for the Americans in the

Press Censorship Department of the Supreme Headquarters Allied Expeditionary Force, and the Certificate of Merit he received at war's end is the earliest official document I have containing his anglicised name: Herbert Garfield. If it hadn't been for Hitler, I would have been Simon Garfunkel.

He qualified as a solicitor in 1947, and he was a partner by the time of my birth in 1960. Four years later we moved from East Finchley to a large house in Hampstead Garden Suburb, and we remained a happy and secure family enjoying middle-class comforts in a confident country. It is not altogether trite to suggest that in the 1960s you could measure the state of a country from its postage stamps. Certainly this is how I learnt much of my history, and it was how Britain wanted to be seen: proud of its past, secure in the present, sure of its future. Battles, Democracy, Heritage, Christmas and always Royalty – these were the regulars, augmented by Science and Technology, Sport and Art. This was my miniaturised encyclopaedia: by learning the background to the Joseph Lister centenary, the building of the Forth Road Bridge and the Emmeline Pankhurst commemoration I would begin to grasp a little of our history. Because new stamps were always an event in those days, their photo in the papers would always be accompanied by a summary of what they were commemorating, and my dad liked to read them out: 'Joseph Rowntree, the confectionery maker and philanthropist, was born in York 130 years ago. Joseph Lister, who developed antiseptic and sterilisation, was born in Essex 140 years ago' – and thus began my journalistic instinct for the meaningful anniversary. These British stamps of the 1960s, always my main interest with errors or not, have never been surpassed, the perfect balance between design and subject matter. There was such a clear order to them, and I remember counting the weeks and days to the next issue. I queued up with my mother and brother at the post office in Market Place, the quaint shopping strip that couldn't bear to think of itself as part of the North Circular, and we were in the company of many other boys and older collectors. Some had brought small stock albums to carry their purchases home flat behind glassine strips. Some had labels to place softly on the corners of first day covers, special envelopes supplied to carry the new stamps with a postmark from the first day of issue.

The stamps were one thing, the buying process another, and adding them to your album at home another still, and I soon came to learn that stamp collecting was rich in rhythms and protocol, and it was this that soon became addictive, the deep comfort of ritual. Looking at them now, they carry a still beauty and clarity: stamps marking the first flight of Concorde and the Jodrell Bank radio telescope, stamps commemorating the 900th anniversary of the Battle of Hastings and the 700th anniversary of Simon de Montfort's Parliament, stamps depicting British birds and wild flowers and famous ships. I've mentioned that I thought this was my history, and in an immediate sense it was. But it was never my family's heritage. My parents never collected stamps, and if they had collected Germany when they were young they would have long abandoned their hobby.

England had welcomed my parents with opportunity, and they took every opportunity themselves to embrace English culture. They loved the stately homes and the old universities, my father loved the rigmaroles and privileges of the legal system, and in the summer of 1966 my mother went mad for Geoff Hurst. Jack Rosenthal couldn't have written it better: England v. Germany in the final, my mother allergic to football for her entire forty-one years, but then suddenly they kicked off at Wembley and she was screaming at the television as the goals went in. Mother 4, Nazis 2. And then a few days later we were at the post office before it opened for the England Winners stamp. I think she bought a whole sheet and used it as regular postage, her own victory lap with Bobby Moore every time she licked one.

As the 1960s progressed I became a more serious collector, and the more I thought of myself as a committed philatelist, the more eager I became for some acknowledgement of my commitment. But as I edged towards my teens I was also growing aware that collecting stamps was not the sort of thing that would bring instant approval from girls. It would not even bring instant approval from boys, and, at a less civilised institution than University College School in Hampstead, philately might have resulted in a beating. The first time I entered my school's annual philatelic competition (which, for the winner, meant a prize on Speech Day, enabling some people in the hall – perhaps my parents – to believe the prize had something to do with academic merit rather than just steaming things off old envelopes), I was not at all surprised to find that the other entrants were the sort of boys I looked down on – the friendless, the ungainly. I didn't envy their lives, just their stamps: one boy, also called Simon, had a small collection of George V 'Sea Horses', high-denomination stamps that, although postally used, were probably worth a hundred pounds. I think he had been left them in a will, something that as far as I knew would never happen to me. For the school competition one year I put together a fairly elaborate story surrounding the Wild Flowers set of 1967, describing each of the flowers in turn and where they grew. I think I listed some varieties I had seen in magazines, such as 'missing campion bloom'. The other Simon mounted his Sea Horses on clean album pages, labelled them 'George V Sea Horses, 1913, 2s 6d, 5s, 10s and £1', and won.

I think the teacher who judged, probably a collector himself, thought the other Simon's stamps worthy of space in his own collection, whereas my flowers he probably had as full sheets, ordinary and phosphor (the phosphor was an innovation to aid automatic sorting).

It would have been unusual for me not to have thought for a minute about stealing the other Simon's stamps. Not because I wanted them, but because I wanted him to be unhappy. The thought quickly passed: I'd be found out, I'd be expelled, I'd still feel unsatisfied. It was at this point that I came to terms with one of the great universal collecting truths: no matter what you had in your collection, it wasn't enough. You could collect all the Queen Elizabeth issues, but there would always be new ones every few weeks, and a gnawing feeling that there were some rare shades or misperforations you didn't yet have, and what about going back to the Georges and Edward VIII and sixty-one years of Victoria? And could you really call yourself a collector if you didn't have something or everything from the Cape of Good Hope and the British Commonwealth? In this way stamps taught me about setting boundaries and limiting one's ambitions – about life, really – but unfortunately this knowledge didn't quell the overriding desire to obtain more stamps.

At school we all put our acquisitions in albums by licking tiny translucent 'hinges' and sticking one bit on the stamp and the other on a page, a process known as mounting, something which instantly reduced the value of mint items by about two-thirds. Not that value was ever the thing. I never collected with an eye on investment, because nothing I could afford cost more than the price of the stamps over the counter. I probably entertained the hope that when I was older the worth of my collection might be able to buy me a car, but I think I knew in my heart that the moment I bought the Battle of Hastings strip, the very first in my collection in 1966, it would probably be worth about the same for years to come, or much less if you separated each of the six stamps from the six-stamp strip, which I did. And then again less when I mounted them, and then less still when I only bought the strip of 4d stamps and the 6d value, and not the 1s 3d key stamp because it seemed too expensive. I know now that 14,865,204 of the ordinary 4d Hastings stamps were sold, and 2,643,660 of the phosphor printing, which means that after almost forty years, these stamps are worth about the same as I paid for them, and I can't even use them for postage.

Occasionally I would buy cellophaned packs from WH Smith that bulged in the middle. These cost a few shillings, and promised to contain stamps with a catalogue value of £5 or £10, which told even an eight year old that catalogue values were not things to rely on. Some packs came with plastic tweezers and a plastic magnifying glass, so that a beginner could pretend to be a pro, much like a child could play with a fake plastic driving wheel in the back of an Austin Allegro. But it was laughable to imagine that the magnifying glass would actually discover anything interesting in that pack of cheap stamps, and the tweezers were redundant too, as you could have handled the stamps with treacle on your fingers and not reduced their value further. The best stamps were ones that came free on envelopes through the letterbox. Franking machines were not yet in every office; secretaries were dispatched to buy two hundred stamps at a time, and even the most official mail had a colourful corner. These would be steamed off with a kettle or placed in warm water, and then dried on newspaper, and they filled a lot of album space.

Once, I sent away for something advertised in the back of a

comic called 'approvals', a fateful snare. The idea of approvals was that you sent away for stamps 'on approval' and only once you had received and 'approved' them did you send back a postal order or cheque as payment. In theory, I suppose, you could have approved some stamps and kept them and rejected others and sent them back, haggling with the dealer about how much was owed; or that at least may have been the implication in the *Dandy*, *Look & Learn* and *Treasure*. But when I sent away for my approvals I had no idea what the concept meant – only that the prospect of receiving expensive-looking stamps with no outlay was appealing.

A free Penny Black was sometimes offered just for sending away, yours to keep whatever you decide. It wasn't clear, at this initial stage, that the Penny Black would have one or no margins, be heavily obliterated, and definitely ruined in other ways. This would be worth hardly anything compared with a three- or four-margined example. (In the days before perforations, the margin showed where it had been cut from the sheet, and the postmaster doing the cutting had no concern for posterity. Which explains why a used strip of six Penny Blacks with excellent margins recently sold at a specialist auction house in Holborn for £90,000.) The advertisement would also have a panel to select your special interests: GB, Commonwealth, Rest of World. And there was a box to confirm that you were over sixteen, or that you had your parents' consent. Tick!

A week or so later, some beautiful stamps would arrive in a stiffened envelope. At least, they looked beautiful. I didn't know this at the time, but they were stamps that had already been sent and rejected by many other collectors, examined by eyes more knowledgeable than mine, and with more sophisticated watermark detectors. Some of them were good but common. Other were less common but probably flawed in minor ways – a short perforation, a thin, a crease. But they looked fine to me at the age of ten or eleven, and I kept the lot. The information sheet that accompanied the stamps – from Empire Services, Congleton, Cheshire, with the come-on lines 'As you inspect these grand stamps and marvel at the low prices we are sure that you will agree that they will make your collection the envy and admiration of your friends'; and the instructions – to 'Take your time. Look through the whole selection several times before deciding, read the fascinating descriptions and carefully take out the stamps you purchase'; and the baffling but key detail, 'Enclosed on 14 days' Approval' – went straight in the bin.

The boys' magazines were full of similar allures for the young collector. One could, for instance, buy something substandard called the Universal Stamp Outfit. This cost 12s 6d, and contained mainly useless and cheap items, but there were ten of them: Bounty stamp album, stamp finder, landfinder, full-size nickel-plated steel tweezers, magnifier (two-inch handle, almost unbreakable), watermark tray, 1,000 hinges, 'How to organize a stamp club', wallet with strip pockets, 1s pack Grand Mixture.

One month after my approvals arrived, there was a follow-up letter. 'We are delighted you have chosen to accept the full card of stamps. The total is £3 15s.' My father sent a cheque, and stopped my pocket money for a while. I think the stamps are now worth about 75p.

Not long after his first heart scare, my father faced another crisis. One of his clients had objected to the way he had handled his case. He may have considered some of my father's advice unwise, or he may have just objected to his fees, but he decided to take the case to the Law Society, and my father faced an extended period of agony under the shadow of suspicion before matters were resolved. He may have taken an enforced holiday during the investigation; I certainly remember the aura of ruin over us, although I'm sure this was exaggerated. The early 1970s was still a time when professional shame could be as final as death; it wasn't something easily finessed away by publicists, or something you could 'use' as celebrities do today. As far as I knew, and I have had many confirmations since, his reputation was immaculate. He was a gentleman in all his dealings, never underhand, always scrupulous. The case eventually went away – either dropped or won by my father – and normal life resumed. But the saga almost certainly affected his heart.

Almost all the memories I have of my father are loving. The only painful one is being hit on by backside with a slipper when I misbehaved. In his eyes I misbehaved often – I think I was always too loud for him, too keen to kick balls inside the house – but I don't think I was beaten more than five times. He really did say 'this hurts me more than it hurts you', but that was just his guilt speaking. My mother hated it when he whacked me, and I think she asked him not to, but it was clearly how he had been brought up, and he thought it had worked well enough for him. What really worked for me was avoiding being hit again by concealing things. Once, when I had broken a small garage window one morning during the school holidays, my mother colluded.

'What can we do?' I asked, fighting back tears.

'You could run away!' she said. But instead she called a glazier, paid him in cash, and the putty was still hardening when my dad drove past it to the end of the garage that evening.

I remember his fondness for cigars, especially during long sessions on the lavatory on Sundays with the papers. I can see myself reading my homework to him in his study on Sunday evenings. I remember him being vaguely disappointed with some of my school reports, and occasionally saying, 'Is this what I spend all that money on?' But he was also very kind and loving. Because I was born when he was forty-one, we didn't have many of the traditional bonding mechanisms. He didn't like music apart from classical ('Really, is that a boy or a girl?'). He didn't like sports apart from golf. We didn't play football in our garden or on Hampstead Heath extension. He did take me to my first Chelsea game, and I recall a midweek evening encounter with Spurs, walking up the steps of the old West Stand at Stamford Bridge to the lush turf and that great/foul smell of cigarettes and burgers and damp coats, and sensing that he was nervous. It wasn't the fear of violence, which was a particular feature of Chelsea games in the early 1970s, it was more of a class thing. I'm not sure my father had been called 'mate' since he left the army. Football was not yet a middle-class pursuit, even in the seated section; this was no place for a Jewish professional from Hamburg, not with the Nuremberg-style arm movements and all that talk of Yids.

To make up for these shortcomings, he had a habit of taking my brother Jonathan and me on holiday in August by ourselves. One year it was him, the next it was me. The only one that sticks is a very wet week in Bournemouth. It rained incessantly for seven days, and we ran between taxis and cinemas and the pier and our hotel, and once I found an antique shop which sold old stamp magazines. I spent hours studying obsolete prices and rare items. I had bought my Gay Venture album, and spent afternoons putting things in. 'Yes, a Gay Venture indeed to every enthusiast,' the frontispiece proclaimed. 'For there is no more enthralling and exciting hobby than stamp collecting . . .' I believed this. '. . . The only one that can interest you whatever type of person you are.' I'm not sure what my dad was doing while I was reading this and mounting. He was probably reading and working on his caseload. 'And if the pictures themselves ever begin to bore (which we doubt), then the search for completion, the chasing of scarce and hard-to-find items, and the study of the stamps themselves as fascinating miniature pieces of printing carry on the interest.' Fatal words.

That was also the year of the muddy rock festival. Not Glastonbury but Reading, grown bearded men turned into reeking brown sculptures suffering from trenchfoot. My father, who had seen real trenchfoot and would never pay for it, thought the world had gone totally mad, but I just cut out the pictures from the newspapers, put them in a scrapbook, and called it my school project.

When he went golfing he sometimes took me along as a weedy caddy. The joke in his foursome was that I always knew the ideal club for the particular shot at hand, but this was usually after he had whispered in my ear '2 wood' or '9 iron'. I would then accidentally pull out a 3 wood or an 8 iron, and he would sometimes believe I had overruled him. I was happy to tag along as his friends talked work or politics or Israel (Jews welcome here in Hertfordshire, or at least tolerated, unlike our local golf club in Highgate). There was usually a Heart ice-cream at the end of it as I joined my mother at the clubhouse pool.

We did play board games together, and with some success. The usual things – Monopoly, Scrabble, Buckaroo (obviously my dad didn't play Buckaroo) and Cluedo, which baffled my mother so much that on one occasion she actually shouted out, 'I did it!' Our favourite was What Am I Bid?, an auction game. The Hamlet cigar adverts were at their peak in the late 1960s, and in one of them a man was at an auction, scratched his nose at the wrong time, and ended up walking home with a stuffed bear as an orchestra played 'Air on a G-String'. We hummed that throughout What Am I Bid?, a simple quest to amass a more valuable collection of antiques than your opponents. This was achieved by bidding on items of furniture (a Chippendale chair, a Sheraton bureau bookcase), porcelain (a Meissen dog), silver (Queen Anne teapot) or something oriental (a Tang period pottery horse). An auctioneer, who was usually my father, would place a picture card on the supplied auction stand, and I, my brother and my mother would bid for it in a desire to complete a category set. The auctioneer ended the auction with a commanding drop of his gavel, and the winning bidder would then discover from the back of the card whether they had won a 'good' example (worth £2,000 in the case of the Meissen dog), a 'poor' one (worth £500), or a fake (£40). There was also a Rarity card in each of the categories, described in the rules as 'an item so rare that it has not been recognised and so miscatalogued'. When one player had obtained three good objects in any one category they could end the game by declaring themselves 'a collector', the ultimate accolade. It was a game I often won, and I think my father helped me by letting me know by a wink or hint when an item he was offering was a fake. In the time when the game wasn't in play, the gavel would have a life outside the box, often used to hammer in nails and kill ants.

We also played a lot of Collect: A Great New Stamp Collecting Game (made by Stanley Gibbons in 1972). This too was a game of risk and uncertainty – did you want to swap a card in your hand, each denoting a stamp from a certain country or theme, for another of unknown category in a desire to build up a better collection? The winner would be the first to build a set of ten stamps in any one group – GB, USA, Animals or Famous People – but if you went for the Rare set you only needed five. One went around a board having good or bad experiences – 'Lose two stamps', 'Special transaction'. The stamp cards had a little information about each issue, designed, I imagine, specifically to appeal to a young mind with an insatiable appetite for facts: 'This is one of a set of six stamps depicting British Wild Flowers, issued in 1967. The design, by the Rev. W. Keble Martin, author of "The Concise British Flora in Colour" . . . the square-rigged, 16th-century galleon, formidable man-o'-war or merchantman, was of Spanish origin.'

I still have the game, and I am struck by how all the instructions describe the players as 'he', and how three drawings of a dark-haired round-faced boy seemingly spellbound by the game look like me. It is also clear that the game was a propaganda exercise for Stanley Gibbons: 'Stamp collecting is a fascinating hobby that has captured people's imagination from the first,' the game's instructions begin. There is information about the formation of Stanley Gibbons in Portsmouth, and how to avoid falling prey to less reputable dealers with fakes. There is also the line that no doubt drew me in more than any other. 'On some recent British stamps where the Queen's head is reduced in size to form a small part of the design, examples are occasionally found with the head missing. Needless to say, these command a higher market price than the normally printed stamps of the same issue.'

And there was another reason why the stamp world was calling to me. The box and instructions feature an enlargement of the Penny Black, with the letters in each bottom corner denoting S for Stanley and G for Gibbons. But I took the initials to be mine.

The only thing my father collected was cigar labels. Or

rather he slipped them off each weekend for me, and I flattened them out and placed them in a stamp stockbook. I probably had about a hundred different types with the pictures of Cuban heroes and emblems on them, but then the collection foundered when my dad found a cigar he really *liked*. The boxes they came in were useful for storing stamps that had yet to be mounted or swapped.

The low cholesterol salt didn't save him, naturally. And neither did the disappearance of the plump Montecristo No. 2s and H. Upmanns, replaced by slim panatellas and Hamlets. Less smoke, same addiction, same awful outcome give or take a few months. Not that I knew there were only to be a few months, no more than he did. And if we both knew there were only a few months, what would we have talked about? Nothing of great value, I imagine. I didn't really understand that having one small heart attack meant that a large one was usually a matter of time. But what do you do with something terrible waiting in the wings? You certainly don't usher it in, and you can never say goodbye in advance.

On 26 November 1973, a damp Monday six weeks after the Yom Kippur War, twelve days after the royal wedding, two days before the Christmas stamps appeared, with my father aged fifty-four, I got home from school and probably did the usual things: a bit of homework, a bit of *Nationwide*. Almost certainly I listened to my Grundig – *The Navy Lark* perhaps, *The Clitheroe Kid*, John Peel playing 'Cindy Incidentally'. And then the following morning I was aware of hushed panic, and my mother not herself, and being told dad wasn't well and I should get off to school as usual, packed lunch, Golders Green to Hampstead Tube, sweets on the way. The usual day at school. And then home to be greeted at the back door by Jonathan, eighteen.

'Dad died.'

I remember saying, 'What?', and was aware that what I said then would be of significance. It wasn't really a question, it was more 'He can't of.'

'This morning. It was sudden.'

I think I said, 'Oh no.' I entered the kitchen, and the world of Jewishness surrounded me like foam in a cavity wall. There was already some food there, supplied by a friend; it was probably traditional 'mourning food', something sweet. Soon other people began appearing, and wished me 'a long life' (trad, Jewish) and said that at least he hadn't suffered much (trad, humane), and already there were details of the funeral the next day or the day after (again traditional Jewish – the swiftest burial possible allowing for Sabbath and other obstacles).

My mother was sitting on our beige velour sofa in the lounge, sobbing with her back to me as I entered. I put my arms around her from behind and she started sobbing more. Eva, my mother's sister, was flying in from Israel. The front door was open even though it was cold outside . . . people on the phone . . . a rabbi being contacted . . . arrangements.

They had married in June 1952. They had known each other in Germany as children, and were very distantly related cousins (before their marriage they had sought advice as to whether their union would present any problems at childbirth, and they were assured not). As my father entered the British army my mother entered the 'Department of Antiquities' in Jerusalem as a trainee archivist, and she qualified not long after the declaration of Israeli Independence in 1948. A few years later she flew in to London for a wedding reception, and my father – who she hadn't seen for at least a decade – picked her up at the arrivals lounge. She looked like Audrey Hepburn, and I imagine they fell in love on the drive into town. They were engaged and married within a few months.

There were condolences, for me and for her. Hers took the form of a great many friends offering all sorts of support – financial, legal, shopping, cooking. She would never be short of advice or love and – in the future – suitors. My father's death was something from which she would never recover, but initially I didn't feel so bad about it. It was just something that happened to people, and I think I found it quite interesting. This was clearly a removed emotion, a way of coping, a profound isolation. It was also something slightly journalistic; to figure out what was going on I remained heartbreakingly outside the reality. Even at the age of thirteen, I wondered if I wasn't using the situation. I was intimately involved in the grimmest of stories, but a story nonetheless. The work I liked doing most involved getting as close as possible to a story over a number of months in an attempt to get to the bottom of it. But you never do.

My main condolences came in the form of the letters sent to my mother. Most of these began, 'It was with deepest sympathy and great shock that we heard the news about your great loss.' They always went on (and who hasn't written the same?) 'Words cannot convey/words alone are insufficient to/I cannot possibly sum up . . .' But they still wrote, because that's what one does; even in the age of text and email, we still write letters of condolence. Inevitably the best ones arrived last, from furthest away. Switzerland, France, Israel, Canada, United States and Africa, all stamped. I tore off the corners of the envelopes with my mother's permission, and began to steam them. The biggest haul I ever had.

Later I learnt that my father had died alone. My mother had called the doctor, and the doctor had thought that my father needed medicine. He felt unwell in the night, felt worse in the morning, but it wasn't anything terrible yet. His heart was sounding all right, presumably. So the doctor departed, my mother went to the chemist in Market Place or maybe Golders Green with the prescription, and by the time she returned it was all over. My father had suffered a fatal heart attack. She had been spared the final paroxysm, and in the grief that followed we considered whether this was all for the best.

My mother may have begun to die at about this time as well. Her cancer was diagnosed in hospital in 1974, but she had self-diagnosed it at least two years before. It was the classic thing of the age: I'm sure she knew what the lump meant, but she lived in fear of the mastectomy and the fall-out. Better, perhaps, to ignore it, not to worry everyone, perhaps it will stabilise. But in the dark, for certain, the truth was always there: it would never go away, it would only spread. She didn't tell me about it as I grew up and it grew harder. I'm sure if she had told my father he would have hastened her to hospital. It spread for two years, until its size, or the fear, or advice from others, compelled her to go to the experts.

Of course this was in the days before routine scans and *Woman's Hour* Specials, the days where the patient felt themselves at fault, and with limited hope of survival after diagnosis. The blunt treatments – surgery, radiotherapy and chemotherapy, the slash, burn and poison with which we have become sickeningly and unwillingly familiar – had improved markedly since my mother was young, but the prognosis of two or three friends had shown her how they sometimes delayed, seldom stabilised, never reversed. In the mid-1970s, ICI was just bringing tamoxifen to market, and, following her mastectomy, my mother was an early trialist.

We stayed on in the big house after my father died, and my mother cared for her two sons and went to work as an assistant at an old-age home near Kenwood in north London. Jonathan and my father's friends helped her with the task of family administration – the bills, the insurance, the taxes, all that upsetting maelstrom from which she had remained insulated – and she became stronger and independent. The cancer retreated for a while.

Her regular check-ups were held at the Middlesex Hospital in Mortimer Street, central London, some two hundred yards from the Post Office Tower. This was also the place I was born. From her consulting room you could see the restaurant revolve, though it had ceased to be open to the public since a bomb, probably planted by the Angry Brigade, exploded in a women's toilet in 1971. Following one consultation in the summer of 1976 we did what we always did – a trip to the Boulevard Restaurant in Wigmore Street for what they called an 'open' smoked salmon sandwich, in other words not a sandwich at all – and then we did something unusual: we did the Strand.

My mum had no interest in stamps whatsoever, but the results of her blood tests had probably been good that day, and she was in an indulgent mood. I hadn't devoted much time to my collection for several years, and I still didn't have much money, but we were celebrating not only clear results but the end of my O levels and a downturn in the heatwave. I felt an expensive present coming on.

Our first call was the post office in Trafalgar Square, the best philatelic counter in London. There were only new stamps on sale here, but the people behind the counter understood the collector's demands. They understood them a lot more than my mother did, and as we queued up I did my best to explain the latest thing in British stamps – gutter pairs.

'Gutter pairs are when two stamps are separated by a strip of white paper. There are ten gutter pairs in every sheet of one hundred stamps, and the gutter, which is also perforated, runs down the middle of a sheet.'

'What's the point of it?' she asked.

She had me there. 'I think it has something to do with the printing process. Or the folding process.'

'But what's the point of collecting them?'

'The point is, they are rare. The early ones are getting very expensive, though I'm not sure why.'

The man behind the counter didn't have much of an idea either, but he knew they were in great demand. The post office in Trafalgar Square was the only place in London I knew where they didn't sigh if you asked for particular strip or block of a stamp sheet. The person in the queue behind the person being served understood too, and never tutted when the wait was long. In fact, the Philatelic Bureau may have been the only queue in Britain where the person behind was genuinely interested in the business being transacted ahead. Ah, you collect cylinder blocks . . . and traffic lights . . . and blocks of four. An addict loves an addict.

What I didn't say, because I had no knowledge of it at the time, was that gutter pairs were something of a scam. They were a way of creating value out of something which, not long before, had only face value. The reason that the early ones were getting expensive – they began appearing with the Silver Wedding issue of 1972 – was because a few dealers had found they had vast amounts of sheets of stamps that no one really wanted, and they conjured a market for them out of thin air. Their adverts in the stamp magazines had a gold rush element to them. 'Special Offer!' one of these ran. 'We strongly and whole-heartedly recommend the complete unmounted mint collection of Great Britain gutter pairs . . . a total of 182 stamps . . . special offer . . . normally over £135 . . . price per collection: £95!'

The key to gutter pairs was the traffic light gutter pair – the one pair in any sheet with the central white strip featuring a small check dot of every colour used in its production. You would not get this for £95, and not even for £900. These days, more than thirty years later, you can find all the traffic light gutters for £100, and the regular ones for a few pounds. It didn't take long for people to come to their senses and realise that what they were buying were two stamps when they only needed one. The Post Office did nothing to discourage this.

'I'll have one of everything you've still got on sale please,' I said to the man behind the counter. 'The Telephone set, and the Social Reformers, and the American Bicentennial and the new Roses set. All in gutter pairs.'

'What do you like about stamps?' my mother asked as we walked up the Strand. This was a tough one, too. I liked their colour and design, and the fact that one could collect them, and the fact that they could be worth something. I don't think I articulated the thought at the time, but I now realise that collecting is about family. Collecting stamps is particularly about family. With stamps one follows a tradition handed down, and one makes new additions, and the boundaries and conventions are fairly well established. Deviate from the norm and you're in trouble; people frown; societies will shun; you'll have trouble selling on. Albums are like homes – ordered dwelling places, and when they become too small to contain the collection we buy something else, something bigger. We begin with the grandest ambition but then downsize; we find what makes us happy and pursue that. We hope that a big family and a big collection will see us through old age.

The good news was, the Strand was the one place where stamp collecting needed no theorising. Here, it seemed like the most natural thing in the world; if you weren't collecting, what on earth were you doing in this street? In those days there seemed to be a stamp shop every ten yards. The Stamp Centre was there, incorporating several specialist dealers. Bridger & Kay and Vera Trinder were close by in Bedford Street, W. E. Lea was opposite in John Adam Street. On a Saturday the treats began much earlier, at the market underneath the Arches by Charing Cross. Here I could afford a few spacefillers and commemorative issues that appeared before I started collecting, including the 1957 World Scout Jubilee Jamboree and the 1962 Ninth International Lifeboat Conference. And I still have the secondhand magazines I bought for a few pennies each. *Stamp Magazine* contained articles headlined 'Postmarks, Places and People' and 'International Reply Coupons – New Design!' There were also articles specifically for beginners on the meaning of philatelic terminology, like *tête-bêche* (two or more joined stamps, with one upside down) and advice on how to look for priceless stamps on old documents in grandma's loft. This would have been fine if grandfather hadn't got there first, and sold anything half-decent to dealers or friends. By the time I began collecting in the 1960s, the world had got wise to the value of stamps. Philately was more than 120 years old, and lofts had long given up their treasures.

I think my mother was always in an indulgent mood when we went shopping together. I also thought that I was her favourite, and that we had the most in common. One of the most memorable things she said to me and about me – and she said it a lot – was that I had good taste. Whenever anyone says this it usually means that you have the same taste as them, and in the case of my mother and me this was true. She liked to take me with her when she shopped for a party dress, and I would give her the nod or the shake. It was like something you see in romantic comedy films – two girlfriends having a ball in a store in New York with one of them in love and the soundtrack at full promo as they giggle over something low-cut and exorbitant. That was me, as one of the girlfriends, although my mother couldn't wear low-cut after 1974. She had a heavy foam sponge which she moved from bra to bra; unless you knew, you wouldn't look twice. On one occasion when my dad was still alive, he had given her money to buy herself a new ring for her birthday. I must have been eleven or twelve, and rather than choose something himself, he would send me out with her. I've still got that ring, bought on holiday somewhere, an impressive jagged gold number like an almond nut cluster, and I still like it.

I can't remember if I bought anything on that stamp trip beyond the new issues. Probably not, as even then I felt that it was something I should do alone. I think I would have been embarrassed to spend even £5 on something she couldn't appreciate. Subsequently I visited the stamp shops with my aunt Ruth, and it was a bit easier with her; she didn't really like stamps either, but she was a bit splashier with her money and was less resistant to impulse. But stamps were private things for me then, and remained so for thirty years. I think I still felt ashamed of the money spent and the pursuit in general, of the lonely hobby with all its misfit connotations.

I was also frightened. I was lost in a world of experts. I didn't believe I would be deliberately cheated, but I feared I would cheat myself. I would be offered a vast choice of Penny Reds from the 1860s, and I'd be bamboozled, and I'd leave the shop in a shaming panic. I had a basic catalogue, but it was far too crude a compass to steer me through so many subtleties of shade and printings and plate numbers and postmark cancellations, all of which affected price. I would have been dissatisfied with any purchase; I could never afford the best, and it pained me that someone somewhere – actually, almost everyone everywhere – owned a better example.

The one place that tried hardest to dispel this feeling of helplessness was Stanley Gibbons, but I found it had the opposite effect. The weight of its history was imposing, and its main showroom, with its ornate ceilings and gilt cornices, far too grand for a shop. The staff tried to entice young collectors with a huge selection of accoutrements; even if you couldn't afford the stamps, surely the pocket money would stretch to a tin of hinges and a set of Showguard mounts. Or perhaps tweezers, or one of the new albums with names from nowhere: The Number 1, The Gay Venture, The Improved, The Safari, The Swiftsure, The Worldex, The Devon, The Exeter, The Plymouth, The Abbey Ring, The Philatelic, The Senator Standard, The Utile Standard, The Oriel, The Windsor, The Tower, The New Imperial, The New Pioneer, The New Thames, The Strand, The Nubian. They were all unbelievably similar.

Gibbons occupied several shops towards the Aldwych end of the Strand, and when you walked into any of them – which took some guts for a sixteen year old, it was like entering a shop selling game-shooting guns or cigars – a man would approach with sudden confusion on his brow: part of him wanted to patronise, and part of him wanted to respond to a missive about encouraging the young, they are our future. Patronising got him: 'And what can we do for the young master today?'

'Um . . .'

'For the young sir, what are your specialities?'

I think I wanted to spill something. It was much easier buying stamps in packs at WHSmith. In Gibbons my stammer worsened. I wanted to look at their stock, but like many stammerers I found that the hardest words to say were those beginning with 'st', such as stock or stamps. 'Just looking,' was all I would usually manage. My mother was no help. 'It's a funny name, Gibbons,' she said. She also wondered whether I would be better off collecting coins; they were older, less likely to get damaged, and in your hand they felt like something.

Gibbons was a funny name, I agreed, but over the years I had got used to it. I told my mum the story of its founder as best I knew it; some of it was quite possibly myth, but certain elements, like the episode with the sailors and the Cape Triangulars, had been told so many times that they had become true. His full name was Edward Stanley Gibbons, and the first photograph of him, possibly from his late teens, shows a bulbous nose, receding hairline and a set of wild side-whiskers. He was born in 1840, the year of the Penny Black. He began collecting in the mid-1850s, encouraged by his father, a chemist. Yes, encouraged: at a time when most people threw every stamp away, and when almost every professional man would regard collecting stamps as a habit of the deranged, William Gibbons allowed his son to section off a part of his chemist's shop and start swapping with like-minded friends. This was in Plymouth; there weren't many.

But the idea of stamps was growing. By 1856 more than twenty countries were issuing stamps, and among the most attractive were those from the Cape of Good Hope. These were triangular, and at their centre a woman reclined on an anchor. They were printed initially in London by Perkins Bacon, the same company that produced the Penny Black, and they became desirable not only because of their shape, but also because of the many variations in shades and impressions from subsequent woodblock printings. In 1863, two sailors approached Gibbons in his shop with a sack containing many thousands of these stamps they said they had won in a raffle. Gibbons bought them for £5, and by the time his first price list appeared two years later he was charging up to four shillings each. In this way he began as he wished to go on: rare stamps, rare prices. He sold his business for £25,000 in 1890, by which time its catalogues had established themselves as authoritative checklists for the world. The buyer was Charles J. Phillips, key supplier to the collector Count Philipp la Rénotière von Ferrary.

My mother showed a vague interest in all of this, but she had other things on her mind, and I don't think we went shopping for stamps again. Occasionally at home she would show me a stamp on an old document from my father's study. Most legal papers were paid for or sealed with stamps, the simplest form of taxation. 'Is this a rare one?' my mother would ask. But it never was.

When I look at my modest collection of GB errors I feel comforted. Whenever I open the album I am delighted with the beauty of the tiny objects, and wonder about their journeys from the printing press to my albums. Because I only collect pre-decimal, the stamps transport me to a time when my father was still alive, and when my life seemed secure. The value of the stamps is an entertaining side issue, and collectors are not being honest if they claim that the cost or worth of their hobby never crosses their mind. But it is the quest for the stamps that keeps us going, not their investment potential. The rising value of rare stamps ultimately becomes a hindrance to the collector rather than a benefit. But still I think: if only my father had helped me invest £1,200 in errors in 1973. How wealthy would I be now? And how happy?

As I think about my father dying, and my mother struggling

with cancer, I find a new reason for my interest in collecting. Postage stamps offer one way in which we may order a world of chaos, and they have the power to bring a dependable meaning to a life. Owning a piece of history – however common, however rare – may even create a fleeting purpose in this world. I don't like it when people just call them pieces of paper.

Imaginings

The first book I can remember reading was a large illustrated animal alphabet – A for Antelope, B for Baboon. E was probably Elephant, Z was Zebra. But X? I think the book said it was for a Fox viewed from behind. It is linked in my mind with Hilaire Belloc's cautionary verses, which often involved the misbehaving being eaten, and with T. S. Eliot's *Old Possum's Book of Practical Cats*, especially Gus the Theatre Cat. These were probably read to me by my mother. I don't think my father read to me at all. Then there were Aesop's Fables, also about animals, and, almost inevitably for a boy of German descent, Struwelpeter, that ultimate shock-haired frightener with bleeding fingers. It was a very moral list: if you did this tempting but terrible deed, it was certain that far more terrible things would happen. It was not a literary world of guilt; it was one of retribution.

My other favourites, the Famous Five and Billy Bunter, held different fears. The dappled summer orchards where the Five resided when they weren't solving mysteries seemed to me an unusually threatening place. The lack of adults made me wonder what had happened to them, and how they would cope on their own. What would they do for money and hot food when the weather turned? I was unsettled by their all-over sunniness, and I knew that within the fields they trampled there would be things waiting to sting you. About that time, at the age of six or seven, on a lonely summer camp in Somerset I ripped my knee on barbed wire climbing over a gate. My hairless leg streamed with blood, and a white scar remains after numerous scabbings and peelings and eatings of the gritty congeal of blood, new skin and iodine. My compensation was extra white bread with strawberry jam. Billy Bunter wasn't so lucky. His mishaps usually ended in a clobbering by bullies and cries of 'yarooh!', which was 'hooray' in reverse. And such was the ending of *Billy Bunter and the Blue Mauritius*, the first book I ever read about stamps.

First published in 1952, when a boy's stamp dreams were big, it was among the first of Frank Richards's Bunter novels. I quite liked Bunter and his greed and laziness, and the fact that, whichever book you happened to be reading, his long-anticipated postal order still hadn't turned up. The arrival of his postal order would solve everything – debt, hunger, inequality – much like the arrival of Bono does today. I also liked the heaving sexual possibilities suggested by Bessie Bunter.*

Billy Bunter and the Blue Mauritius tells the preposterous

---

* And what I would have liked even more, if only I'd known about it, was the fact that Frank Richards was not the author's real name, and that Charles Hamilton (for that's who he was) had other aliases too, and that together all these *noms de plume* wrote a book about every six weeks. This is not much of an exaggeration. As himself, Hamilton wrote almost thirty novels between 1908 and 1940 – titles such as *Chums of the South Seas* and *Rivals of Treasure Island*. He wrote one book as Michael Blake, one as Prosper Howard, two as Owen Conquest, five as Winston Cardew, twelve as Ralph Redway, around thirty as Martin Clifford, and almost eighty as Frank Richards. At one point he changed sex to Hilda Richards for the Bessie Bunter volumes. You certainly wouldn't want to be organising his launch parties. In 1930 he published eight titles, and in 1946, a year of strict austerity, there were ten. After his death in 1961, at the age of eighty-five, he somehow

and compelling tale of the theft, several times within a couple of weeks, of one of the rarest stamps in the world. The plot is not just unbelievable to philatelists, but also to Bunterists. Long before I knew anything about stamps I understood that anything valuable – and in this story the Blue Mauritius is valued at £2,000 – has to be kept securely in great condition. I knew how much my father valued the ornaments in the sitting room by how tightly I had to sit on my hands. So it would not do to carry a rare stamp carelessly around damp woodlands surrounding Greyfriars school, and it definitely wouldn't be worth £2,000 if it had been jammed for days inside Billy Bunter's pocket-watch.

But of course this was schoolboy fiction, and I lapped it up. The tale begins regularly enough, with Bunter puffing his way towards school, almost certainly late for 'roll', but two very brief chapters later we are ensconced in caper. The Fat Owl has lost his way and fallen asleep in the woods, and is woken by the desperate shouts of Sir Hilton Popper, the local baronet. Sir Hilton is still wearing his pyjamas under his coat, and is in pursuit of a man who has stolen his Blue Mauritius in the small hours. This stamp cost him £500 in his youth, and was now the 'exhibition piece' of his collection, or at least it was until some bounder made off with it. Bunter manages to collide with the

---

managed to publish from beyond the grave. And then there were his plays and lyrics, including the songs 'What's the Matter with England?' and 'Tell Me, What Is Love?'

It is not clear why he had so many names. What is clear is that Charles Hamilton's oeuvre is highly collectable en masse, especially the French translations. First editions of some of his books never became second editions, which render them particularly sought after. My Bunter collection, which was the first collection of anything I ever owned, once had pristine covers, and in the collecting world condition is everything. But then they were thrown away or lost, and the only one that remains is the one about stamps.

thief in the dark of the woods, and Sir Hilton gets his stamp back. But is he grateful? No, he is not. He chastises Bunter for trespassing.

A while later, with Virgil homework complete, Bunter is once again in a thicket with his five chums. And there again is Sir Hilton Popper, and they can just make out an income tax demand in his pocket and a scowl on his face. Sir Hilton, 'a gentleman whose estate was covered by mortgages almost as thickly as by oaks and beeches', owed the Revenue much money, and had taken to talking to himself as he worked out the solution. 'How is a man to meet such demands?' he wonders. 'Last year I had to sell a farm! The year before to let my house to a bounder. This year I must sell the stamp.'

Bunter and his friends are not philatelists, but when Sir Hilton removes the Blue Mauritius from his pocket-book, 'They realised . . . that it was something special and precious in the postage-stamp line. They were able to discern that it was blue in colour, and that it showed a profile of Queen Victoria. They also caught the words "Two Pence".' Frank Richards was probably no philatelist either, or he would not have had Sir Hilton pick up his stamp between finger and thumb rather than tweezers, and certainly not directly after a lamb supper. Almost inevitably, it isn't long before the stamp is stolen again.

I would follow these exploits lying on my bed. My bedroom had a good-sized desk for homework and model-making, a row of shelves by the door with young novels and Guinness fact books, a pinboard by a window with Chelsea posters detached from *Goal*, and a view that looked into a wide leafy street and sideways towards our elderly spinster neighbours. My bed had a built-in storage unit along one side in which I kept the things that were dearest to me – Grundig radio and cassette player, magazines, a bear, my small stamp album. I was relieved to sleep here every night rather than the boarding school dorms of my fiction. (At one point my shelves also held the Moomintroll books by Tove Jansson, and one of these, *Finn Family Moomintroll*, carried the impossibly sad woe of the Hemulen. The Hemulen moped around at the start of the book because he had completed his stamp collection and now had nothing to do. 'There isn't a stamp or an error that I haven't collected. Not one.' It dawned on Moomintroll what a tragedy this was. 'I think I'm beginning to understand . . . You aren't a collector any more, only an owner, and that isn't nearly so much fun.')

By a satisfyingly improbable sequence of events, Bunter again finds the Blue Mauritius for Popper at the end of the book, and Popper rewards him with a beating for not finding it sooner. Six weeks later, Bunter is again waiting anxiously for the postman in *Billy Bunter's Beanfeast*.

The story of the stamp went on. The next time I encountered it, it was in an American crime thriller and I was in London's Finchley Road. Between the ages of thirteen and fifteen, the corner shop next to Frognal railway station was a valuable source of soft-core pornography, and many boys at University College School would call in there on the way to or from the playing fields. Storage was no problem: you can bury a lot of things in a dank Puma holdall and the external bat sleeve of a cricket bag. It was the usual fare – *Club International*, *Men Only*, *Health & Efficiency* at the last resort – and we passed them around the pavilion with a nonchalance we would later use on teenage girls in our gangs at Golders Green and Hampstead: we are only vaguely interested, we shrugged, when we were all very interested indeed. Inevitably, we ran on to rugby and cricket pitches exhausted. It was also that phase at an all-boys school when we were as interested in each other as in the magazines.

The shop in the Finchley Road had two sections, the section at the front which had nothing anyone was interested in, and the damp section at the back, beyond a sticky plastic rainbow curtain. We were so underage, but the owner was obliging and understood. With school friends that curtain was no barrier at all, and we'd swan through on a mission. Most of the magazines had been previously owned and dispensed with, and they had an earthy smell. Occasionally there would be a cache of Americans – *Hustler*, *Twink*, *Superjugs* – none of them hard-core, but somehow more exotic, more unreachable. The further away the women in these magazines were, the safer I felt. And in the American magazines there would occasionally be men with huge drooping penises, perhaps photographed after the act, an act perhaps appearing in another magazine yet to make it to NW3.

There were rarely any women I actually fancied in either the American or British mags, and of course I would have been profoundly nervous of any real-life encounters. The Readers' Wives, all old enough to be my mother, were particularly unattractive and overgrown, and taught me something subliminal about the dangers of bad lighting. Georgie from Berkhamsted likes to party. Pamela from Northholt likes to join her. But where were these places, and where were these parties? One of our number, a boy called Steve who had sprouted early and claimed to have learnt to drive in a field, also claimed to have done it with a girl in a phone booth on holiday, and the rest of us were both suspicious and jealous.

His story never changed. It was 'delustful', he said often, 'very delustful'. I'm not sure I have ever heard anyone use this word since. 'And cramped,' I should have said. Instead, I thought about what could have gone where, and whether she sat on the metal phonebook shelf, and how cold that could have been.

'Mary was gorgeous,' Steve said. 'Long blonde hair . . . nipples like cherries.' He was, almost certainly, describing a film he may have read about, probably starring Mary Millington or the impossibly sized Chesty Morgan. The nearest I got to a real mythical girl was by calling the numbers in the back of the magazines. There would be many promises: many 'lessons', some 'punishment', all of it 'strict'. I thought I had suffered enough of that at school, but I was enticed by pictures of blondes with their hair back and their mouths open, and so I phoned them. I think I knew I was being ripped off with my very first call. One could never actually reach Bernadette or whoever, not because she was still running from her catechism tutorial to be with me, but because she was completely imagined by, I imagine, an unusually fat man from Essex. I would get a certain way each time. 'Very shortly you will be put through to Bernadette, who is panting to meet you,' informed a soft female voice. 'But first . . .' But first there was some nonsense about holding the line while a technical problem was solved, and then there was a delay while a new phoneline was advertised with the promise of triple-X fare, and then Bernadette would be along any minute now, and then there was a recorded tape of someone calling me a big boy until the line went dead. It was so convincing, and my hopes so high, that I must have called at least three times before I realised that this was a technical fault that was more complex than first thought. And then because Bernadette wasn't available, I would try Susan or Carole.

I had no idea how much these calls would cost my parents, but we lived in that blissful era before bills came itemised. I would call when they were out in the evenings and I was being looked after by my brother. I wouldn't tell him what I was doing, but he would have understood; I later found a small but neatly arranged pile of magazines at the bottom of his bedroom cupboard. They were *Parades*,* cost 8p at the dawn of decimalisation, and I have them in my dubiously titled 'rare publications' box along with first copies of *Whizzer and Chips*, the *Face* and the *Independent* (there are none of my own 'glamour' magazines in there, as these were recycled into the eager school pool or thrown away on Hampstead Heath with shame).

A few weeks went by, and then an unexpectedly large phone bill arrived in Hampstead Garden Suburb, and my parents may have put this down to an increase in the price of their calls to their relatives in Israel. For the next few weeks my family in Tel Aviv and Jerusalem would wonder why things had gone silent our end, unaware that I had been financing someone's white-shagpiled mansion in Basildon.

In the Finchley Road, there was another conundrum: how to enter the back of the shop by myself. As part of a gang, the plastic curtains were all swish swish swish behind us. (*Swish*: wasn't that another magazine of the period? Caning?) But by yourself, the eyes of the owner were upon you, as were the eyes of everyone walking in the street towards Swiss Cottage or Golders Green. It looked almost like a regular bookshop from the outside, even though few of the books in the window had actually been published in the last decade. There were a lot of sporting and show-business autobiographies, a lot of

---

* You could quite feasibly get away with buying a copy of *Parade* without shame, and read it going home on a quiet bus, learning why Joe Mercer 'Wouldn't Take a Back Seat' and taking up the offer to 'Win a Set of Tools'. There may even have been people who genuinely bought the magazine for the articles, the way people claimed to buy *Playboy* for Norman Mailer. *Parade*, of course, did not have Norman Mailer. It had Owen Summers on Crime ('From This Phone Box a Killer Called') and John Stanley on Motoring ('Watch It – Wankel Power Is Coming'). Every issue contained three or four spreads of naked women, thank God.

almanacs. But as you emerged from the shop with something new in brown paper in the holdall, everyone passing knew you hadn't bought *Swingin' Dors* by Diana Dors. The gulf between the regular books, laid out like meat products in a 1970s Moscow supermarket, and the innards of the Swish was so vast that even Hannibal would have thought twice. The owner had no problem with a teenager indulging in the Swish; indeed we were his best customers. But his attempt to put a young, lone, uniformed blusher at his ease only made things worse.

'Good afternoon, Sir.'

I had only been called 'Sir' in gentleman's outfitters and in stamp shops. In fact, the similarity between buying porn and buying stamps was only just becoming clear. The slight seediness, especially in the early 1970s; the feeling that, at all times, you were being conned; the impression that there was always something better that you weren't allowed to see; the unshakeable belief that no matter how long you looked, you would never be satisfied.

'Is there anything I can help you with?'

This was in the front, legit part of the shop. I always said I was just browsing, which was true, but how many times can you flick through *Hunt for Goals* by Roger Hunt? I was, of course, always looking towards the Swish, and the shop owner knew it. I think I only made my solo way through there twice, and the rest of the time I just dawdled. One day the legitimate shelves bore a new cache of crime thrillers. These were probably by James Hadley Chase, Erle Stanley Gardner, Eric Ambler and Ngaio Marsh. But I was taken by the work of Vernon Warren, and one book in particular: *The Blue Mauritius*.

Here was that stamp again, an object more desirable than the red-headed broad being held at gunpoint on the jacket (the spine of the book showed the Blue Mauritius with a silver dagger through it, probably also not the work of a long-term, serious philatelist). The plot was distinctly hard-boiled, and a lot like Mickey Spillane. It was full of girls called Mitzi. At the start of the book, a private detective is down on his luck when an unlikely-looking client walks into his cold Chicago office. 'For a hobby I practise the art of Philately, are you with me?' the stranger asks.

'You collect postage stamps, yeah I follow.'

At this stage – the book was published in 1954, two years after Bunter – the stamp is valued at $20,000. But the stamp the client mentions is rarer still, predominantly because it only exists in fiction. Rather than a twopence blue, it is a one-penny blue. It was an error. It should have been a one-penny red, but the dyes got mixed up. According to the stranger, only one sheet was printed before the error was noticed, and all but one stamp was destroyed. This is now worth more than $150,000. And had the stranger ever seen the stamp? 'Seen it? I've owned it.' The problem was, he had needed some cash, sold the stamp, regretted it almost instantly, and now had enough 'simoleons' to buy it back. Ah, if only things were that easy. The new owner of the stamp won't sell it even for $450,000, and the stranger has gotten desperate. 'Do you realise what it is like to own something when it's the only one in the world?' he asks the detective.

'No, mebbe I don't.'

The stranger asks the detective to steal the stamp back for him, but the fee the detective wants – $250,000 – is too steep. They say goodbye. And then the adventure really starts, with the detective travelling to New York to track down the dealer who bought the stamp from the stranger, and then the man who bought it from the dealer. Only problem: the man who bought it has been murdered . . .

*

As a stamp collector, the Blue Mauritius follows you to your grave. More exotic than the Penny Black and a hundred times rarer, it is a stamp so heavy with lore that its true history outflanks its fictitious appearances. Any account* will describe the story of the glamorous ball held in Port Louis in 1847 by the Governor's wife Lady Gomm. The envelopes used for the invitations marked the first ever use of the one-penny orange-red and the twopence blue, and in so doing established Mauritius as only the fifth country in the world to issue stamps. The twopence stamp, which was modelled on the British Penny Red but was of far coarser design, carried an inscription on all four sides: Postage, Mauritius, Two Pence, Post Office. These days a British colony stamp would probably carry a picture of an indigenous species, or an extinct one, which in the case of Mauritius would have been the dodo. In 1847 it was a badly drawn portrait of Queen Victoria with something approaching a double chin. It is believed 500 were printed of each value, but only twenty-six or twenty-seven are known to have survived. The stamps continued to be worth twopence (or less because they were used) until about 1865, when a market for them was established by French collectors. As Detective Brandon was informed by the New York dealer he met on his travels, the stamp has 'no legal value whatsoever . . . the immense value that attaches to it is given only by the few specialists for that kind of thing that there are in the world'. This is the essence of all stamp collecting, indeed of collecting anything: you don't have to be one of the Duveen brothers to know that a stamp, like everything else you may purchase at auction, is only worth what someone is prepared to pay for it.

Part of the initial allure in France – apart from the fact that

* The most recent and accessible is *Blue Mauritius* by Helen Morgan, Atlantic Books, 2006.

these stamps were a vivid fresh discovery in a flourishing new hobby – was that it contained the words 'Post Office', whereas the stamps printed from an improved engraving the following year in far greater numbers bore the words 'Post Paid'. It was also very rare, as the vast majority were thrown away in Mauritian waste bins well before new ballgowns were ordered for Lady Gomm's party (1,000 'Post Office' stamps were printed in 1847, whereas it is believed 100,000 of the 'Post Paid' stamps were printed between 1848 and 1859). And in this way the stamp became a holy grail. One 1d used stamp surfaced in 1869 in Bordeaux and was sold to a female dealer named Madame Desbois. It was then bought by Moens along with some other stamps, who sold it on to a collector for about £10 in 1870. In 1897 a dealer bought the stamp as part of this man's entire collection, valuing it at about £1,200. In 1901 it was bought by the Berlin Reichspostmuseum, where it was placed in a glass-fronted display frame, surviving the Second World War first in the museum's vaults and then in a mineshaft in Eisleben. In 1977, a year after a former US army soldier had offered the frame for sale to the London philatelist Robson Lowe (who reported this offer to Interpol), the soldier surrendered it to the US Customs Service. Following reunification, it was returned to a postal museum in Bonn, and it is now on display at its new permanent home (until history pulls it away . . .) in the Museum für Post und Kommunikation in Berlin. And no doubt those who see it report its bearing as 'luminous', for nothing adds ardent light to a stamp better than a brilliant past.

One twopence specimen, unused, slightly damaged and repaired, followed a similar route from Bordeaux to Madame Desbois, and then to J. B. Moens. Moens sold it to Count Ferrary in 1875, for 600 francs (about £24). In 1886 Ferrary swapped the stamp with T. K. Tapling, whose collection was bequeathed to the British Museum after his death in 1891. This was the one that really caught my eye.

Tapling and Ferrary were the two giants of nineteenth-century collecting, and they couldn't have been more different. Tapling was seven years younger, educated at Harrow, a Member of Parliament, a cricketer (he played one match for the MCC), fond of cravats. Though born to good stock and great wealth, Ferrary was practically feral.

He was born illegitimate in 1848 and brought up in Germany and France. He began collecting at the age of ten. He was a serious boy, and a sensitive one: he reportedly suffered a great deal when he heard of the humiliation inflicted upon the Austrian armies by Napoleon III at Solferino. His ancestors were also collectors, and their main interest appeared to be collecting money. His maternal grandfather, a Genoese banker, was said to have died of starvation when he deposited himself in a vault with his gold but failed to take the key to let himself out. The banker's daughter, Ferrary's mother, the Duchess of Galliera, was only given the key to her husband's private library shortly before he died, and when she entered she found a great many shelves of bound volumes containing government bonds, some £12 million in total.

And so it was, at the death of his mother in 1888, that Count Ferrary found himself suddenly able to acquire all the things he dreamed of as a child. His inheritance was $25 million. What he dreamed of was something every modern collector can never dare to dream – the feat of completion. With the possible exception of the King of England, no one else would ever entertain such ambitions again. Ferrary was to be thwarted in his aim: even in 1888, forty-eight years after the Penny Black, it was already impossible to collect everything. Even if you had the money, some things were just not available. But Ferrary tried.

He had several important dealers, including J. P. Moens and Pierre Mahe, the latter becoming the keeper of his collection in Paris as he travelled throughout Europe on his quest for more stamps. He desired to buy every unique and legendary rarity in the world – the five-cent dull-blue Boscawen Postmaster stamp; the Kiautschou five-pfennig double-printed with 5fP rather than 5Pf; the 1851 Hawaiian two-cent blue, the 1856 British Guiana one-cent black on magenta, the Swedish tre-skilling banco of 1855 (yellow, error of colour, the only known example that wasn't the intended green).

Like most collectors, Ferrary thrilled as much to the chase as the conquest. He bought them every way you can imagine and a few more besides, paying far over the odds to happy dealers. At one stage he owned four copies of the Blue Mauritius. The stamps were housed at 57 rue de Varenne, in a private wing of a palace occupied by the Austrian ambassador. His collection was rarely seen by visitors, but one who did gain entrance was Charles J. Phillips, another of Ferrary's principal dealers. He described a room covered on three sides by cupboards with shelves, the shelves containing 'stamps all mounted on strips of stout paper'; they were not in albums but in bundles organised alphabetically, and some of the bundles were distinctly dusty. Elsewhere there were tall piles of discarded albums and paper sheets containing the unwanted duplicates from the many collections he had purchased to plunder a few rare specimens. Behind Mahe's desk stood a board with banknotes nailed to it in various denominations: 50,000 francs was allocated each week for the purchase of new stamps. At one stage in the 1890s, Ferrary's relatives became so alarmed at the amount he was spending on stamps that they decided to use the French courts to slow him down. His relatives claimed he had gone insane; to prove otherwise, Ferrary enrolled in a law course at the University of Brussels, obtaining his degree after five years. He also gave his 'solemn word' that 'in no case and under no pretext whatever I would make a debit and never purchase anything for which I could not pay cash'.

According to a book by Gustav Schenk,* the Count never found peace during his work on the ultimate collection; he must have realised that he could never get it all, and he didn't know enough about his quarry to value them beyond their monetary value. Accordingly, he was preyed on by scam artists who prepared fakes specifically for his visit. These stamps, unique in themselves, are now known as Ferrarities. But there is some evidence he knew what he was doing. He once spent a large amount with a dealer in Berlin, and on his return to Paris he was informed that almost all of his purchases were duds. 'Do you think I had not seen that?' Ferrary is reported as asking. 'The man wanted money badly, and had nothing else, so I had to take the forgeries.' On one occasion he bought an item from the known forgers Benjamin and Sarpy as it was being prepared in the back room.

Ferrary's zeal and compassion hinted at a singular ambition: immortality. 'The philatelic memorial to which I have devoted my entire life', he wrote in his will, 'I bequeath with pride and joy to my beloved German fatherland.' He was writing in the middle of the First World War; he died in 1917. He had once hoped to leave his GB and Colonies stamps to the British Museum, where they would have sat alongside Tapling's, but the war changed his plans. His stamps, which he wished to be known as the Arnold Collection, were seized by the French as war reparations, and auctioned at various

* *The Romance of the Postage Stamp*, Jonathan Cape, 1962.

sales between 1921 and 1923. The sales provoked feverish bidding, and many items reached record prices. Bidders came from all over the world, attracted not only by the rare lots, but also by the stories attached to them. The total value of the sale was £402,965.

Throughout my new stamp frenzy, it seemed that every publication I picked up had stamps in it. Count Ferrary would have been pleased with *The Plot against America*, the 2004 novel by Philip Roth, and certainly he would have loved its jacket. This displayed a one-cent stamp with a pleasant green image of Yosemite in California, or it would have been pleasant had it not been overprinted with a heavy black swastika. The novel imagines a scenario in which the isolationist Jew-baiting Charles A. Lindbergh had defeated Franklin Roosevelt in the 1940 election. Another nightmare occurs early in the book, when the young male narrator has a dream that his prized set of 1934 National Parks stamps have all been vandalised with the swastika. Earlier in the dream, the portrait of George Washington on a set of stamps had been replaced with that of Adolf Hitler. Stamps are everything for this seven year old; inspired by the widely publicised collecting passions of Roosevelt, he carries his stamp album with him everywhere, much as other children his age carried teddy bears. I had no trouble imagining myself in his shoes.

A short while after reading this I picked up a copy of *The New Yorker*, and there was a short story by Louise Erdrich called 'Disaster Stamps of Pluto'. Pluto is not the planet (as was), but a backward town in North Dakota. The narrator takes a walk with her friend Neve, who tells her that her uncle Octave, who recently drowned himself in a shallow river, used to collect stamps.

'Do you remember stamp collections?' Neve asks the narrator. 'How important those were? The rage?'

The narrator says that she did remember, and that people still collected stamps.

But Octave was not just any collector. He was the Ferrary of his day, a collector with everything. He kept his stamps in Pluto's bank vault, and it was worth as much as the bank's entire cash stock. He had the tre-skilling banco from Sweden, the British Guiana one-cent magenta, the one-cent Z-Grill – anything monumental in the stamp world, Octave had scaled it, and put it in one of his fifty-nine albums. But that wasn't enough for him. 'My uncle's specialty', Neve explains, '. . . was what you might call the dark side of stamp collecting . . . My uncle's melancholia drew him specifically to what are called "errors".'

Yes, Octave collected stamps with missing text and missing colours, but he also collected crash and burn mail – mail that survived big disasters like the *Titanic* and the *Hindenburg* and Pompeii. Unfortunately, Octave took it all too far: he began to forge his own disaster mail, and that proved a disaster for Octave. After her uncle's suicide, Neve decided to sell his collection and move to Fargo.

The characters in the short story then discuss the upside-down airplane stamp, the most famous error of all. In 1918, the US Post Office issued a set of three stamps to mark the beginning of its domestic airmail flights. Each of them featured the Curtiss Jenny biplane, but only the twenty-four-cent value was printed in two colours, dark blue (the plane) and carmine (the frame). The two colours required that the sheet of one hundred stamps be pulled through the printer twice, and on one occasion the sheet was passed through the wrong way round, resulting in the 'Jenny' appearing upside down. The man who bought the entire sheet over a post office counter in Washington DC knew the value of this great find immediately, and refused all offers until he found the promise of $15,000 from a business consortium irresistible. The sheet was immediately sold to E. H. R. 'Harry' Green, an obese millionaire with a cork leg who periodically opened the door of his car on New York's Nassau Street and made the dealers come to him. The sheet was long ago split into blocks of four and singles. In May 2002, a collector bought three of the blocks for $2.5 million.

I would go for a drink with friends and someone would mention a stamp book they had read as a child. The poet Ruth Padel said I should look up a novel by Robert Graves – *Antigua, Penny, Puce*. I was pretty sure she had made a mistake. I knew some of Graves's work, and this didn't sound like his sort of thing at all. Besides, there was no such stamp. But here it is with me now, a book written in Majorca, the one Graves calls his only 'light' novel, about a brother and sister fighting over the ownership of a unique stamp. It is not vintage Graves. It is not even vintage stamp literature, for it crawls along like a heavy Balearic afternoon, not like Bunter or the Brandon thriller. But it does contain one bullseye passage. 'All British schoolboys of a certain age collect postage stamps,' Graves wrote in 1936,

or at least all schoolboys whose parents have a little money; below a certain social level the collecting instinct must, we suppose, be satisfied largely with cigarette pictures and gift-coupons. Schoolgirls, on the other hand . . . schoolgirls do not go in for stamp collecting. In fact, they usually despise the pursuit, which is not direct and personal enough to satisfy them emotionally: if they collect anything it is signed photographs of famous actresses and actors. But they have brothers, and brothers collect stamps. So in the holidays they very often consent to lend a hand in the game. They rummage in bedroom drawers, and in their parents' writing-desks, and in boxes in the attic, and sometimes make quite useful hauls. The brothers are touched and gratified. Schoolgirls are not interested in stamps, agreed, but – this is the important point – they are undeniably interested in their brothers' preoccupation with stamps. What is it all about? What is the sense of it?

These are good questions. But the key thing about this passage is the observation that collecting is an instinct. It is not whether one collects, it is what.

Almost everything from my bedside table has gone. Indeed, apart from my first stamp album, almost everything from my bedroom has gone. But how do we agree to these departures? What confident error of forward thinking allows us or our mothers to dispose of childhood property, or secure it in a loft never to be retrieved? How can we tell, at the age of twelve or thirteen, that we will not one day miss these things?

My Dealer

When I returned to stamps in my early forties I found that the market had changed. The Strand was no longer the Mecca of philately, and was unrecognisable from when I had last examined it with a collector's eye. Gibbons and the Strand Stamp Centre were still there, but the weekly Saturday market had gone, along with many traders. A few had retired and sold up, a few had gone bankrupt, and others had just decided to work from home and send catalogues in the post. Then the Internet came along, and they didn't even have to spend postage any more.

One shop that had disappeared was owned by a man named David Brandon. Brandon had opened for business in 1975, and during my first collecting phase I had marvelled at the treasures on display. Brandon sold almost everything – GB across all reigns, British Commonwealth, most of the world, albums and many accessories such as watermark and phosphor detectors. The shop was there for eleven years, until Brandon realised that he could do without paying the high property rates and would probably sell just as many stamps to his regular clients via mail order.

To attract new clients, and remind people that he still had a knockout selection of stamps, Brandon now placed advertisements in the monthly magazines. Along with his son, he had developed a new speciality. 'Honesty, Integrity and Confidentiality,' proclaimed one advert in *Gibbons Stamp Monthly* not long after I had taken up collecting again. 'We believe that these are the three most important words when choosing a dealer to help you build the Great Britain Collection of your desire. Being the world's leading and most active dealers in Important Investment Quality Errors we would be pleased to hear from you, should you care to obtain major pieces such as the items illustrated.' The items illustrated included the Jaguar with the missing Minis, and the Red Cross stamp without the red cross. Another advert appeared in July 2004 announcing another twenty major pieces, ranging from a George VI *tête-bêche* mis-cut booklet pane to the 1967 Wild Flowers with missing agate. Just four sets of this existed, and Brandon had the only complete block of four. According to the advert, the block was last offered for sale by a man called Derek Worboys, and had remained in a private collection ever since. The price was £8,500.

I found the pictures of the stamps irresistible, and so I called up and bought three modest things. I selected the items with great care, and all of them were classic but common stamps I remembered from childhood: 1965 Joseph Lister Discovery Centenary 4d missing brown-red, 1966 British Birds 4d black-bird missing legs, 1966 World Cup 1s 3d missing blue. This was the beginning: you start small, you like the experience and the product, you get hooked. I had a good conversation with Brandon about prices and great errors, and we hit if off straight away. He knew the area where I lived quite well from his pre-stamp days, and it emerged that we also had a shared interest in the history of the London Underground. Then he did what I considered a remarkable thing: he sent me the stamps I had asked for without first receiving my cheque. It was like getting 'approvals' again, only this time I knew what I was doing, or thought I did. I knew David Brandon was someone I could trust. But he almost certainly knew that by sending me the stamps without prepayment he was establishing an obligation. Three modest errors were never going to be enough. I sent him a cheque for £1,200 immediately, the stamps arrived (in perfect condition, carefully packed between two pieces of stiff corrugated plastic), but I could have received them as a gift, and Brandon still would have profited. You get that at druggy parties – the first hits free and within a week you'd pay anything for more. In that simple three-stamp transaction the error world was pulling me back in.

During one of our conversations, Brandon said I should come down one day if I was ever in the area. I could see no prospect of being in the area at any time, but I really wanted to see more of his stock, and so we fixed a date for lunch. He sent me an email: 'Dress casual, have a relaxing time.'

Before I drove to his place, I bought some more stamps. They were beauties, though not the rarest. I bought a block of four 5d ships from the 1969 issue that sold more than 67 million; mine were missing black, which meant there was no Queen's head, value, hull or inscription, and were four out of seventy-two known. I also got what was technically called a 'wild' perforation on a block of Battle of Britain stamps, which meant that the printed stamps had somehow got caught up in the perforating machine and were cut at unique angles. And then, for £2,000, I bought a horizontal pair of stamps from 1965 that I had been keen on for a while – the ones missing olive-green, the ones without the Post Office Tower.

*

'Value was immaterial to me when I began,' David Brandon told me. 'My plan when I was at school was to have one of every country in the catalogue, but that was when the simplified world catalogue was in one volume not four.' Brandon was sixty-two, small and slender with large glasses, and he was still fond of wearing jeans. He was like no other dealer I had met, in so far as he was someone I wouldn't be nervous about introducing to my friends or my family. He wasn't just into stamps. He also collected London bus and underground maps and tight clothes for his partner Linda on eBay.

He lived and worked on the outskirts of Guildford, Surrey, in a secluded wooded area protected by steel gates and security cameras. His office contained shelves of stamp catalogues and also a large safe with many boxes of breathtaking items. He still deals in stamps from all over the world, but the booming business is in errors.

He explained that when he was growing up in the 1950s every village had a little stamp shop, and everybody collected. '*Everybody*,' he told me again, as he knew it would be impossible to believe. Once a week his mother gave him sixpence to buy stamps from his headmaster's office during break-time, and he also bought from a shop near his home in Barnes (he said he could still smell the smoke from the dealer's cigars). He obtained the last stamp to complete his one-stamp-from-every-country-in-the-world collection in 1960, travelling to Bridger & Kay in the Strand to spend £1 5s on an item from Mafeking. Ever since, he's been collecting Boer War.

His father was an executive at Lyon's Bakery, and when he left school at sixteen he worked for Lyon's Ice Cream. By nineteen he was a sales rep, and his earnings went on stamps. Occasionally he would place adverts in the local newspaper offering items he no longer wanted or owned in duplicate, and he found that the techniques he had honed to sell vanilla blocks could be turned effectively to a new trade. At twenty-one he began dealing in stamps from the back office of a newsagent's his father had bought in Putney. He placed adverts in *Stamp Collecting Weekly*, and soon found that his own collection and dealer's stock became one. 'Occasionally I would advertise something I didn't have,' he told me. 'There was something coming up in auction and I knew that if I could buy it for £20 and sell it for £22 then I couldn't lose. If I couldn't buy it for less than I'd already sold it for I'd just return the money and say, "Sorry, the item's sold." Of course nowadays you're not supposed to do that.'

He stopped doing this not long after meeting a man who advised a merchant bank on alternative investments. From then on he would get telephone calls asking him to buy stamps with other people's money, and he would put a £1,000 portfolio together of classic Canada or Mauritius, making a little profit on the side. 'I was still in my mid-twenties, and nobody knew how I was buying and selling so many stamps,' he said.

His investment friend died in the mid-1970s and his bank was bought, but by then he was already well established at the major London stamp fairs and, with his brother, had converted a dry-cleaner's shop on the Strand. He remembers about forty competing dealers within a few hundred yards, but he had a prime position directly opposite Gibbons. He is still fond of saying, 'No – actually they were opposite me.' He would work hard to get some of Gibbons's trade. 'I don't understand why people bought from them,' he told me, 'unless it was a cheap-ish stamp you just needed to complete a set. But why someone would spend £5,000 on a stamp when they could buy the same stamp from me for £3,500 or £4,000 I don't know – the same quality. There are lots of collectors who believe that because they are buying it from Gibbons it has to be better quality, and of course that's not the case.'

Brandon would spend a portion of every day in his shop disappointing people. Men and women would come in with their stamp albums, or their dead brother's albums, and they thought they might be worth a fortune. Brandon could usually tell what the stamps were worth by the sort of albums they came in. If they were tatty, he would sometimes pretend to weigh them in his left hand and, without even opening the cover, would say, '£20!' Some customers thought he was being serious, and considered the offer with a sigh. Their eyes would lighten a little when Brandon then spent a minute flicking through the pages. Better than he originally thought, he said: £25! The problem was, the inexperienced believed that their stamps were worth what it said in the Stanley Gibbons catalogues, whereas that was merely a top-end selling price, often including a handling charge. The cheap stamps listed in the catalogue at 20p each were actually worth about a penny when you came to sell them. It is only the truly rare stamps that achieve the catalogue price. Every collector learns this lesson early on, and then they have to make a decision. Do they throw it all in as a waste of time and money, or do they persevere? The true collectors persevere, because they are in love. I gave up my hobby for about twenty-five years, but when it came looking for me again I was helpless.

Towards the end of the 1970s, Brandon and his competitors all benefited from a brief philatelic boom. Newspapers began extolling the virtues of stamps not just as a quiet hobby for those who don't get out much, but also as a fertile opportunity for profit, and there was always a story of great finds in an attic and a flabbergasted owner. In addition, many countries operated strict exchange-control regulations, but you could put stamps in your wallet and customs officials rarely bothered you. Several stamps had been singled out for investment potential, including the 1929 George V GB Postal Union Congress £1 and the 1939 George VI high values, and their price rose astonishingly within two years. In 1976, David Brandon was selling a well-centred, excellently perforated mint copy of the PUC £1 for about £700; three years later it was £2,500. This elaborately engraved stamp, which featured St George and the Dragon, is consistently voted the most beautiful British stamp of all time. The problem was, it was a common stamp. The crash came in 1980, when the market was flooded and the auction prices slumped dramatically. The price of a PUC £1 went back to about £500, and those who had bought at the top end just a few months before suffered badly. Brandon was left with fifty-one copies, and took a big loss, but he did manage to carry on trading. 'I've always loved stamps, so pulling out wasn't an option,' he told me. 'But a lot of dealers were buying stamps with an overdraft, and they couldn't sell their stock at a sufficient price to pay off what they owed. So they went down.' In those days it was said that you had to have a particular talent not to be able to make money out of stamps. 'It was thought that so long as you kept buying PUC £1s you couldn't go wrong,' Brandon said. 'These days people realise that you need knowledge.'

Brandon has used his knowledge to build up a profitable sideline: expertisation. During one of my visits to his house, Brandon pointed to a pile of certificates of genuineness he had just done for a small auction house, and he showed me the card of stamps from Bermuda to which they referred. 'That's repaired, that's re-backed . . . that's a forgery, that's a forgery, those are all genuine, that's a forgery . . .' His expertising committee, which consists of Brandon and two others, changes its personnel depending on what is being examined. It has been going since 1976. It grew from the dissatisfaction some dealers felt in waiting four or five months for certificates to arrive from the established Royal Philatelic Society and the British Philatelic Association. 'We'd be interested in a stamp, and perhaps buy it, but then we'd have to wait months for a certificate before we could sell it.'

He told me that he had to handle the stamps to know whether they were genuine or not. 'Then I can give you an opinion which is probably 99.9 per cent correct before I examine it closely. When I first did expertising, I knew someone who could tell by looking at a stamp through a [transparent] envelope. You just know if it's right or wrong. But we get items for certificating that people say they got on eBay, and even before it comes in I know it's going to be wrong. And invariably it is. It costs them £59.92 to find out.'

The majority of the items he examines are genuine. Many of the early stamps have faults – creases and thins – but he says expect things to be a little bit soiled after 150 years. 'But with eBay it's always 99.9 per cent wrong. You get what you pay for, and you don't get a stamp worth £1,000 for £20.'

His certificates leave no room for misinterpretation: 'The Committee is of the opinion that the Great Britain, 1965 (8 October), 3d multicoloured, chalk-surfaced paper, Watermark Multiple Crowns (sideways), Perforation 14 x 15, olive-yellow (Tower) omitted (SG.679a) unused pair with full original gum is genuine.' This is accompanied by a photograph. 'With most of this stuff now,' Brandon says, 'we've seen so much of it over the years that you could almost do it with your eyes shut.'

*

I always learnt a lot from David Brandon, particularly what a good salesman he was. I visited him several times to talk about his life and the history of great stamps and collectors, and at the end of each visit I usually had a quick look at his error stock. There were all sorts of things I had no interest in, and many things I loved but couldn't possibly afford. As I flicked through each specimen on a special showcard, Brandon said things like, 'That's a wonderful example,' and, 'That block is unique – as far as I'm aware, the biggest in the world.' On a couple of occasions I made a point of not bringing my cheque-book so that I wouldn't be tempted by a rash purchase. But this cautionary act was irrelevant. 'You can just take it if you like,' Brandon said as I admired a copy of the 65p Nobel Prize stamp from 2001. I didn't really collect decimal issues (just too many of them), but this stamp was something else. The normal examples had a small hologram of a boron molecule on them. The error had no hologram, just white space on a white stamp with a little inscription on it. These were purchased from a post office in Kent, and there were eight copies known. While I was admiring it he told me that there are a lot of collectors whose partners have no idea how much they spend on stamps. A lot of people say to him, 'Here's the cheque, please don't send me an invoice, the wife wants a new cooker. Just take it if you like,' Brandon said, 'and you can send me payment in instalments.' I'd only seen one in a magazine before. I took it.

And then I took it back. After I had owned the missing holo-gram stamp for a couple of weeks I concluded that I had made a big mistake. The stamp was stunning, and genuinely rare, but it had actually cost me tens of thousands of pounds more than I had realised. The problem was, it wouldn't be a one-off pur-chase, because it was decimal. Previously all my major purchases had been pre-decimal, which was a manageable specialisation encompassing only a decade of commemoratives; after 1971, the field opened up into a vast territory I didn't understand. The pre-decimal stamps were the ones I grew up with, while most of those that came after held no comparable charms. So I called David Brandon on the phone. 'The bad news is, I think I've made an error of my own.'

'It really isn't done', he said, 'to take things back.'

'I was hoping I could trade it for some earlier items, like a block of the 1965 International Telecommunication Union Centenary 1s 6d missing pink.'

'OK, he said. 'Because it's you.'

On one occasion I told him of my passion for the 1s 3d 1961 Parliamentary Conference stamp without the Queen, and he said, 'I know what you mean – it's absolutely beautiful. If I had a dozen I could sell them all by the end of the week.' I asked him what my chances were of getting one. 'You never know,' he said. 'I'll have to talk to Mark.' Mark was his son who now lived in Portugal, and handled the modern errors. 'The problem is,' David Brandon continued, 'you could have all the money in the world, and if a stamp isn't available you can't get it.' He explained that some of his wealthiest clients had spent many unrewarding years searching for stamps with a catalogue value of under £40. With the 1s 3d Parliamentary stamp the dozen examples he mentioned did not exist; there were only six known, and only four in mint condition. With stamps, my dealer said, it's always a quest. 'Any fool can simply write out a cheque.'

On one of my visits to David Brandon's house, I noticed a large collection of stamp albums stored in cardboard boxes just inside his entrance porch. 'Oh that,' Brandon told me a few weeks later. 'I sold that on. There were no rarities, just a big general all-world collection from someone who's been collecting for forty years and who lived down the road. I'd never even heard of them, but his son used to go to school with my son Mark and knew the stamp connection in our family.' Brandon then described the collection with a phrase that put a chill around my heart. He called them 'mostly small nothing stamps'.

Mark Brandon: excitingly, this was the same name as the detective hero in the hard-boiled American caper about the Blue Mauritius I had stumbled upon in the Finchley Road. When I told David Brandon about this – indeed, when I presented him with the book as a surprise – he was delighted. In fact, he couldn't believe it. He flicked through it, marvelling at the other Brandon titles: *Brandon in New York*, *Brandon Returns*, *Brandon Takes Over*. 'I will give it to Mark as a Christmas present from you,' he said, adding, 'It is unbelievable!'

Brandon then took me down to a basement room where he had some rare wine and many old stamp auction catalogues and books. He suggested I borrow a couple, and said there was no hurry to return them. Mostly they turned out to be dull. 'There are lots of books about stamps,' he said, partly as a warning. 'And they don't really sell.' I told him my book was about stamps, but also about other things. 'Well,' he said in search of compensatory phrasing, 'I'm sure your book will sell more than the ones that didn't sell so well.'

I got to know Brandon's son Mark over a lunch of melon and overstuffed roast beef sandwiches at his father's house. He was thirty-six, and built like a middleweight boxer. He was more of a businessman than an obsessive collector, and like most young men eager to make an impression on the world, he was keen to do this in a profession far away from his father's. During school holidays he used to help out in the shop in the Strand, and he collected a few things, but he was never really passionate about stamps. He studied business management at college, and began his selling career in a jewellery shop in Guildford. But then, because stamps can enter your bloodstream and never leave you, in 1987 he got a job behind the counter at Stanley Gibbons. He graduated from selling albums and tweezers to handling stamps, and one day a customer walked in and said he wanted to look at the modern errors. Brandon sold him a lot, and he began to see their appeal. His father had been handling the same sort of errors for years, but now he had discovered them for himself.

Errors swiftly became Mark Brandon's main interest. He thought they were undervalued, but saw that some customers were uncertain of their true worth because there was so little information about them. The head of the Queen may be beautifully absent from a stamp, and only twelve copies may be known, but who was to say two hundred more wouldn't be discovered in the future? There was no specialist catalogue, and occasionally in the Stanley Gibbons catalogue some of the prices were higher for stamps that Mark Brandon saw for sale every day than for those he had only heard about, the stamps that his clients really drooled over. So Brandon became a specialist himself, and after a couple of years he left Gibbons to work in an informal partnership with Derek Worboys, who had the best error stock in the country.

The upsurge in interest and price of GB errors may be attributed partly to the publication in 2003 of a book produced by Mark Brandon and a friend of his called Richard, who also lived in Portugal and preferred to be known under the pseudonym Tom Pierron. *The Catalogue of Errors*, which contained

400 pages and a CD-ROM, was the first comprehensive guide to $QE2$ varieties. To the collector and the trade, this was a wonderful volume, not only legitimising their strange stamps, but attempting to place a market value on them. The value was based not merely on rarity, but also on visual appeal; a stamp missing phosphor bands, of which there were only six known, was almost always worth less than a stamp with a missing value or colour of which there were ten.

The word 'known' is the key one here. The problem with errors has always been that a collector may have what they believe to be one of eight examples on a sheet bought from a post office in Cheltenham, but then it turns out that for ten years some bastard has been hoarding a block of twenty discovered in Truro. Or that someone discovers that a block of four they've had in their collection for twenty years and never given much heed, actually has no green on it. This is unlikely, but the prospect once caused me night-sweats. Tom Pierron's judgement about quantities has relied on his own knowledge as a collector, Brandon's expertise as a dealer, and every anecdote and whisper they could find from old catalogues and magazines and their friends.

In his introduction, Pierron considers the issue of investment. A tactic to consider, he suggests, is buying up as many of a single error as possible and sitting on the copies for a while. Then release them slowly over time to extract the best possible price. It can be a costly and slow process, though. He calculated the approximate value of certain classic errors over an extended period of time, based primarily on realisations at auctions. I almost weep when I report that in 1980, the Parliamentary 1s 3d missing blue was £500. It went up to £900 in 1985, £3,000 in 1990, £4,000 in 1995, £4,500 in 2000, and £6,500 in 2003.

He also included a chart about the quantities of the various types of errors in a particular decade, which shows how the three printing companies used by the Post Office slowly got their act together. In 1960, a year which saw both an increase in the number of commemorative issues and experiments with multiple colours, there were 300 missing colour errors compared with zero in the decade before. In the 1970s there were 143, in the 1980s there were seven, and in the 1990s there were fifteen.

At the beginning of 2005 the second edition of the Errors catalogue appeared, vastly expanded, and it broke many collectors' hearts. The prices of many great items had increased to unaffordability. If you had one of these you were laughing; I felt glum, the sort of glumness that descended from the day I saw the Post Office Tower error as a boy and has rarely lifted since. It's really not the money I could have made, but it's the beautiful thing I could have owned.

Mark Brandon bought Derek Worboys's stock a year before he died. Worboys was planning his retirement, and it was a great shock when, while undergoing routine surgery, he died on the operating table. He did not have the error field to himself – his main competitor was a firm called B. Alan Ltd, and there were several others who sold errors as part of their general trade – but he had the most impressive range (on his website he called it 'the most significant stock of rare stamps on the planet'). I asked him about his clients. One of them, he said, a man called Gavin, had nearly everything, old money and decimal, rare and not so rare. Would he talk to me? 'I can ask him.' (He did ask him, and he said 'no'.) Brandon had told me that most error collectors tend to be terribly protective of their collections, and the last person they would want to discuss it with would be another collector. It might put them at a disadvantage when an item they required came up for auction. It might upset the market if they had taken Tom Pierron's tip and hoarded many examples of a particular stamp. And it might upset their wife or husband (usually wife) to read how much they were spending.

Mark Brandon thought there were about two thousand people who collected GB errors, including about fifty who were prepared to spend many thousands of pounds every year. He said that his errors website regularly attracted ten thousand page hits a day. I wondered what would happen to the market when the current generation died, fearing there weren't enough younger collectors to keep the hobby alive. Mark Brandon thought the rare stuff would always be in demand, and was cheered by witnessing a riot in the Far East when young collectors thought the post office would close before they could get a new set of stamps postmarked on the first day of issue.

We also talked about forgery – the forging of error. The Brandons said that gold Queen's heads can be removed from many stamps with ironing and chemicals, including the 1966 Hastings set, but you can spot that one because the embossing would usually be removed as well. Some pale colours will just change on exposure to light, or after wiping with some sort of solution, but you can spot that with a good ultraviolet lamp. 'Chloramine-T they used to use . . .' David Brandon said.

'You must have made some mistakes over the years,' I suggested.

'Oh, all the time,' Mark Brandon said. 'Everything I sell is too cheap. It's the same story – I wish I had most things I sold ten years ago because they're worth twice as much.' He talked about the Post Office Savings issue. He bought the original block of thirty stamps before it was split up into three strips, and sold it in 1988 for £20,000. If he was to sell that now it would be £60,000 or £70,000. 'But you have to live and eat,' he pointed out, 'so you can't hoard the stuff.'

I told him of my lust for the 1s 3d Parliamentary, and asked what my chances were of acquiring one. 'Not great,' Mark Brandon said. 'Unless you're very lucky and one comes up for auction.'

David Brandon mentioned some of his celebrity customers, including Arthur Negus ('came into the shop a lot, charming gent'), Adam Faith ('a great friend'), Lee Marvin Junior ('looked just like his dad') and Leslie Crowther ('couldn't stand him'). His biggest customer was a man named Sir Gawaine Baillie. I had become aware of him shortly after his death in December 2003. Sir Gawaine achieved fame racing Jaguars and Fords alongside Stirling Moss in the late 1950s, and became wealthy through his company H. P. C. Engineering, which he ran for more than forty years. On his mother's death in 1974 he inherited the estate surrounding Leeds Castle (the Castle itself was bequeathed to the nation) and it was about this time that he rediscovered his fondest boyhood hobby. His obituary in the *Daily Telegraph* didn't mention his interest in stamps, which is some omission, because he devoted four hours each day to his passion, and in the process formed arguably the greatest private collection of modern times. It was valued at about £11 million, and contained items that made even the coolest dealers drop to their knees. His collection showed a mastery of the British West Indies, the Australian States, British Africa and Rhodesia, British North America, New Zealand and all outposts of the British Empire. And then there was Great Britain – the Victorian colour trials and plate proofs, mint blocks of Penny Blacks and Twopenny Blues, a unique sheet of the 1880 2s brown, and the famous 2d Tyrian Plum, which, following the death of King Edward VII in May 1910, was never issued. And then there were the Great Britain errors, including the 1966 Birds block missing black, blue, bistre and reddish brown, and the orange Minis without the Jaguar, which was said to be Sir Gawaine's personal favourite. 'He died far too young, just 69!' David Brandon told me in an email. 'He was an absolutely charming, kind, understanding and altogether lovely man. He had come to my house many times and we had some great days together on stamps.' Needless to say, if ever parts of the Baillie collection came up for sale it would make paupers of all who bid for it.

And within a few months, penury beckoned. Sir Gawaine Baillie had died. His entire collection was to be sold by Sotheby's in ten separate auctions. When the huge and beautiful catalogue accompanying the first sale arrived at my house one morning in August 2004, I made a phone call cancelling a meeting after lunch and retired upstairs with it to my bedroom. On page 224, lot 1061, was the stamp I had wanted more than any other, the 1961 1s 3d Seventh Commonwealth Parliamentary Conference missing the Queen's head. Apart from light wrinkles on the gum, it was a perfect example, a strip of three. There were only four perfect examples in the world. The estimate was £2,000–£2,500. I remember closing the door and spending the next three hours in rapture.

Not Alone

Men and women began collecting stamps in 1840, the same year that stamps began. These days it is easy to regard the earliest collectors as eccentrics and obsessives, more so, indeed, than we may regard the stamp collector in the modern age. But the Victorian collectors were also celebrationists. They were witnessing another great advance in communications, as significant as the birth of inter-city railways a decade before. They knew this because they were the immediate beneficiaries of this transformation. Further, they had helped bring it about: in 1840, the postage stamp was not just an attractive and intricate piece of paper, it was also a symbol of the popular will.

Before the Penny Post, the postal system was reliable but complex and costly; after it, letters arrived not only faster and more cheaply, but in vastly increased numbers. In 1839, one year before reform, the number of letters carried in the UK was 75,907,572. In 1840 the number more than doubled to 168,768,344. Ten years later the number was 347,069,071. How was this done? With foresight and zeal.

In the early nineteenth century it cost 4d to send a light letter from one end of London to another. The same letter would cost 8d from London to Brighton, 10d to Nottingham and at least

1s to Scotland. The prices had been raised frequently to pay for the Napoleonic wars, and varied according to whether they were carried by mail coach or coastal steamer. The Post Office was well organised and managed all but the final yard of the delivery with efficiency. But then there was a problem, as postage was usually paid by the recipient, a slow enough process even if the recipient was available when the postman called; it was like paying a utility bill every day. As a revenue-raising scheme it was first class; as a democratic form of communication it was fraught with difficulty and corruption. Members of Parliament had long resisted reform because the system suited them well: they received free postage on signature, and they accepted paid seats on company boards in return for signing everything that left the company's offices.

As disquiet about these inequities grew, the outgoing Secretary of the Post Office, Sir Francis Freeling, began to feel cornered. In a private note he wrote, 'Cheap postage – what is this men are talking about? Can it be that all my life I have been in error?' He complained that throughout his career he had run the most efficient service possible, and carried out his duties to the letter. 'Where else in the world does the merchant or manufacturer have the materials of his trade carried for him gratuitously or at so low a rate as to leave no margin of profit?'

This would not have brought much sympathy from Robert Wallace, MP for Greenock, elected through the extension of the franchise in the 1832 Parliamentary Reform Act, and a fierce opponent of the current postal service. Where Freeling saw efficiency, Wallace saw mismanagement and delay. His speeches came to the attention of a civil servant named Rowland Hill. With Wallace's assistance Hill conducted his own research into the postal system, and he published his proposal for improvement in that most Victorian of campaigning methods – the pamphlet. Hill noted the abnormalities and corruptions, and showed that revenue from postage had been gradually falling in recent years despite the huge potential profits to be made.

His suggestions were revolutionary. He proposed a uniform postal charge of one penny per half-ounce for any letter sent within the British Isles, and submitted that the cost should be paid in advance. To this end he drew on a previous idea of Charles Knight for a prepaid letter envelope, but his second idea was the one we remember him for: 'A bit of paper just large enough to bear the stamp, and covered at the back with a glutinous wash which the user might, by applying a little moisture, attach to the back of the letter.' Hill's 'stamp' was reference to the proof-of-postage design that had yet to be decided upon; the whole sticky square was known initially as a 'label'.

Scholars and pedants like to argue that others also have a claim on the invention of the stamp – there is a Lieutenant Treffenberg of Sweden (1823), James Chalmers, a bookseller from Dundee (1834), and Laurenz Kosir from Austria (1836). Their claims are well founded but almost irrelevant. It is never difficult, after the event, to claim that you were the one who had the idea for 'Eleanor Rigby' or a boy wizard's adventures at school. By fortune of circumstance and the energy that inspiration brings, Rowland Hill was the one who made it public and made it happen. Despite the haughty air visible in the most popular engraving of Hill, his biographers do not portray him as an arrogant man or even an unduly self-interested one; there is certainly no evidence of stealing another's ideas for credit, and he emerges keenly focused on the common good. Perhaps this explained his popularity. His reforms, which seem to us today both elementary and long overdue, were still a leap into the unknown. People were not used to paying for the postal service in advance; but they trusted Hill and his practical convictions.

Hill envisaged another breakthrough: 'Probably it would soon be unnecessary even to await the opening of the door, as every house might be provided with a letter box into which the Letter Carrier would drop the letters, and having knocked, he would pass on as fast as he could walk.'

Support for Hill's proposals followed in enthusiastic waves as soon as his pamphlet appeared. Newspapers, who saw how much they would benefit themselves, were keen champions, and soon a government Select Committee was calling expert witnesses. Principal opposition arose from the office most criticised by the reformers. The Postmaster General, Lord Lichfield, complained that 'of all the wild and visionary schemes which I have ever heard or read of, it is the most extravagant!', but his voice was lonely and his criticism contained the one apt description of Hill's proposals that we still uphold today: visionary. The House of Commons voted in favour of penny postage in July 1839, and in the Lords even the Postmaster-General announced his grudging support due to 'universal' feeling in the country. A few weeks later, Hill was offered a post at the Treasury, and after a prolonged period of haggling over his salary and the power of his office, he undertook to change the nature of communication.

Hill was born in Kidderminster, Worcestershire, and later moved to north London, where his father ran a school and encouraged his son to consider issues of educational reform. He had no background in postal matters, although his skill at administration had been evident in his job as secretary to the government department that encouraged emigration to South Australia.

He was less skilled in the matter of design. How was the new stamp to look? The basics we now take for granted – the size, the monarch's head, the licking – were all to be formulated. Uniform Penny Postage was introduced four months before the new adhesive labels were ready, with handstamps from about three hundred towns being used in their place. There was an immediate increase in the amount of post through the system, despite some bafflement over the need to prepay. But there was an immediate incentive to grasp the new reforms: prepaid letters would cost one penny, whereas those paid on delivery would cost two.

The Treasury announced a competition to find a design for the new stamp. A notice in *The Times* requested that 'artists, men of science, and the public in general, may have an opportunity of offering any suggestions or proposals as to the manner in which the stamp may best be brought into use'. Particular attention was to be paid with regards to convenience of use, security against forgery and expense, and there were to be awards of £200 and £100.

There were more than 2,600 entries, and although the Treasury committee praised the widespread ingenuity, none were considered exact or desirable enough to pass into production. Four £100 commendations were issued, including one to Henry Cole, who was already employed as Rowland Hill's chief assistant. In the end, the stamp was designed and produced by a group of professional men already known to Hill and the Inland Revenue for their role in the printing of bank notes and other official items. The Queen's head was drawn by the artist Henry Corbould, taking his inspiration from the relief portrait on the City Medal designed by William Wyon. It was engraved by Charles Heath and his son Frederick, while the words 'Postage' above the portrait and 'One Penny' below it were engraved by William Salter. The stamps were printed by the security printers Perkins, Bacon and Petch, on handmade watermarked paper (the watermark was a small crown) supplied by Mr Stacey Wise. The finished product was introduced to postmasters at the end of April 1840, with clear instructions on how the stamps should be issued and cancelled. A sample of two Penny Blacks was attached to the instructions, so that they could become familiar with the new postal currency. They also received an example of prepaid postal stationery, an envelope and lettersheet design by William Mulready containing images of elephants, lions, Britannia and people engrossed in their mail deliveries, an illustration rapidly and widely parodied by London stationers, the parodies themselves forming the basis of many new collections.

The stamps – the Penny Black and the Twopence Blue – went on sale on Friday 1 May 1840, along with prepaid envelopes, and a revolution got under way. They were not intended for use before Wednesday 6 May, although some were issued early. 'Great bustle at the Stamp Office,' Rowland Hill recorded in his diary on the evening of 1 May. On the following day he noted, '£2,500 worth of stamps sold yesterday'. By 6 May 22,993 sheets of 240 stamps each had been issued to 253 post offices, and on 22 May, Hill recorded, 'The demand for the labels is enormous, the printers supply more than half a million per day, and even this is not enough.'

There was a problem almost immediately: the red cancellations issued in a Maltese Cross design were easily removed and the stamps used again. 'All sorts of tricks are being played by the public,' Rowland Hill observed, and much time and effort was spent on finding an answer. Additives appeared on the stamps to hold the ink, and the red ink was later changed to black. But in the end another solution was found: the Penny Black would be replaced in February 1841 by another stamp that would be less open to abuse: the Penny Red. The problem with the Penny Red was, it didn't carry the same weight of history, it was lighter in weight and didn't feel the same in the hand, and it wasn't beautiful.

In 1843 Rowland Hill went to work for the London & Brighton Railway, but he returned to postal reform three years later, and his endeavours transformed the landscape. He campaigned among householders and carpenters to have his letter-boxes installed, he greatly increased the number of roadside posting boxes, and he introduced the concept of London postal districts. By the time of his retirement in 1864, half the world had adopted his reforms; no one, with the possible exception of the railway Stephensons, contributed more to the global communication of ideas.

And beyond this, Hill may be credited with inventing an entirely new hobby. Sheets of Penny Blacks and Twopenny Blues contained 240 stamps, and to limit forgeries and enable the tracing of portions of a sheet, each stamp had a letter in the two bottom corners. The rows running down the sheet had the same letter in the left corner, while the right corner progressed alphabetically. The first row went AA, AB, AC and so on, and thirteen rows down it went MA, MB, MC . . . There were twenty horizontal rows of twelve, so that the last stamp at the bottom right-hand corner was TL. People who got a lot of post thought it would be fun to collect the set.

One of the first mentions of the new hobby appeared in a German magazine in 1845, which noted, much in the manner of comedian Bob Newhart describing Raleigh's attempt to promote tobacco, how the English post office sold 'small square pieces of paper bearing the head of the Queen, and these are stuck on the letter to be franked'. The writer observed that the

Queen's head looked very pretty, and that the English 'reveal their strange character by collecting these stamps'.

The first collector history is aware of was a woman known only as 'E.D.', who is identified in an advertisement in *The Times* in 1841: 'A young lady, being desirous of covering her dressing room with cancelled postage stamps, has been so far encouraged in her wish by private friends as to have succeeded in collecting sixteen thousand. These, however, being insufficient, she will be greatly obliged, if any good-natured person who may have these (otherwise useless) little articles at their disposal, would assist her in her whimsical project.' There were two addresses to send the stamps, one in Leadenhall Street in the City, one in Hackney. There are no further records of E.D.'s collection, nor are there pictures of her room, which must have been a shade on the dark side. These days her room would be bought by Charles Saatchi. By the following year she had competition. *Punch* noted that 'a new mania has bitten the industriously idle ladies of England . . . They betray more anxiety to treasure up the Queen's heads than Harry the Eighth did to get rid of them.'

Stamp collecting as we understand it probably began in the school classroom, practised by schoolboys and encouraged by teachers of history and geography. We have long been familiar with the strange collecting passions of the playground – marbles, soldiers, Batman cards, Pogs, Pokemon – but we should ask ourselves whether the passions are more perverse than the trend observed by S. F. Cresswell, a master at Tonbridge School in the late 1850s. Cresswell informed the periodical *Notes and Queries* that a boy had shown him a collection of between three hundred and four hundred different stamps from all over the world, and he wanted to know whether there was a guide listing every stamp available and a place in

London where one might buy and exchange them. Subsequent issues of *Notes and Queries* offered him no help, but S. F. Cresswell was only slightly ahead of his time, as we know from one of the earliest published histories of the hobby by William Hardy and Edward Bacon. *The Stamp Collector*, from 1898, listed the large number of philatelic societies that had sprung up since Cresswell had first looked for them forty years before. There was the Stamp Exchange Protection Society of Highbury Park, London, the Cambridge University Philatelic Society, and the Suburban Stamp Exchange Club of St Albans, Hertfordshire. There were also societies in Calcutta, Melbourne, Ontario, Baltimore and Bucharest. Hardy and Bacon identified the key moment that always defines the coming of age and ultimate validation of any serious collecting hobby: the publication of a catalogue. This told collectors that they were not alone, and it set the boundaries of a collector's ambitions. *The Stamp Collectors' Guide: Being a List of English and Foreign Postage Stamps with 200 Facsimile Drawings by Frederick Booty* was published in 1862, three years before the price-list produced by Stanley Gibbons. Booty's pamphlet consisted of fifty pages, and begins with a statement observing that 'Some two or three years ago, when collectors were to be numbered by units, they are now numbered by hundreds.'

Within five years of the Hardy and Bacon book, philatelic literature had come of age. At the beginning of the twentieth century, there were not only many books, albums, glossaries and catalogues, but also the surest indicator that there were considerable sums to be made from attaching oneself to the hobby's coat-tails. There were pocket magnifying glasses, many different sizes of ready-gummed mounts, a 'tuck case for the waistcoat', and an early set of tweezers called 'The Philatelists' Vade

Mecum' ('An Entirely New and Original Invention for Enabling Collectors to Mount Stamps without Handling Them, a *multum in parvo* of Philatelic Requisites'). There was what was almost certainly the first philatelic novel, *The Stamp King* by Messrs Beauregard and Gorsse, an adventure in which two rival philatelists set off from New York to find the world's rarest stamp, taking in London, Paris and Naples en route, and recommended by *Vanity Fair* as 'excellently got up' and by the *Spectator* as 'a diverting extravaganza'. As for the availability of stamps themselves, in 1900 one could buy 500 stamps of Europe, all different, at 7s 6d, or 105 from Australia and 100 from Central America at the same price. One dealer offered an impressive all-world collection, already mounted on sheets, of four thousand stamps at £18.

In 1902, the prominent English philatelist Edward J. Nankivell wrote a pamphlet called *Stamp Collecting as a Pastime*, and in it he tried to identify quite what it was that caused the whole of Britain 'and almost all the world' to be in thrall to the mysteries of postage. People 'are thunderstruck at the enormous prices paid for rare stamps, and at the fortunes that are spent and made'. He observed how 'it has steadily developed into an engrossing hobby for the leisured and the busy of all classes and all ranks of life, from the monarch on his throne to the errand boy in the merchant's office'. Nankivell took his cue from physicians: a hobby was good for the heart, and no wonder it was becoming 'more and more the favourite indoor relaxation with brain-workers'. Already, he observed, the pastime had its own bons mots, and the most popular was, 'Once a stamp collector, always a stamp collector.'

By 1902, the debate over whether stamps represented a good investment had established itself on familiar tracks:

Nankivell advised that rare stamps were always a good bet, while almost all of those that emerged mint from the world's post offices would be unlikely to accumulate for many years, if ever. Today this seems absurd, for we know that many late Victorian stamps are extremely valuable, particularly in unused condition; blocks or sheets of high values can provide for a secure retirement. But the author's premise was based on the belief that 'in stamps, as in every other class of investment, the foolish may buy what is worthless instead of what is valuable'. The same holds true today for those who, ensnared by the Royal Mail's literature suggesting that new stamps may be a reliable heirloom, believe that they are buying anything other than intricately designed and elaborately marketed postage. 'There are stamps specially manufactured and issued to catch such flats,' Edward Nankivell wrote more than a century ago, 'and they are easily hooked by the thousand every year, despite the continual warnings of experienced collectors.'

But stamps have always had other values beyond the speculative or the postal. In lovers' hands they are secret codes. In the last few years, letters between troops fighting in Afghanistan and Iraq and loved ones at home would occasionally carry stamps placed on envelopes at unusual angles. A stamp stuck on upside down would often mean: 'My world is upside down without you.' A stamp at a strange angle might signify a kiss. Email, often censored, found it hard to compete with these tactile emotions. The stamp may also conceal a secret message beneath it.

But this is nothing new. Before stamps, as Rowland Hill recognised in his first pamphlet, the paying recipient of a letter could save money by refusing to pay the charge upon delivery, gleaning all they needed to know from the coded markings on the envelope. After 1840, Victorian lovers used the tilting of a stamp to convey elaborate messages, particularly on postcards where only public emotions could be expressed. The less imaginative could buy a preprinted deciphering card to decode the lexicon. Different languages had different translations: in English a stamp tilted to the left often meant 'Will you be mine?', but in German this was read as 'Why don't you reply?'

In June 2007, 167 years since the Penny Black first made history, it made history again. William H. Gross, the supremely wealthy chief executive at the bond investment company Pimco, sold a mint block of twenty-four Penny Blacks for $1 million at auction. The block was actually two blocks – one a block of eighteen stamps, the largest in private hands, running six across and three down, and the other a strip of six stamps that ran along the bottom of that block. The stamps were 'reunited' in the late 1990s, and are as perfect an example of the issue as one could hope to find, with excellent colour, almost full gum and great margins, the left-hand margin of the large block bearing the lettering '. . . ICE 1d per label 1/- Per Row of 12. £1. Per Sheet. Plac . . .'. The bottom block added a 'PR . . .' to the beginning of the inscription, and had the sheet been even bigger the instructions to those who found the use of stamps novel, which was everyone, would have continued '. . . e the Labels ABOVE the Address and towards the RIGHT HAND SIDE of the Letter. In Wetting the Back be careful not to remove the Cement.'

William H. Gross was selling his line-engraved Great Britain collection to benefit Médecins Sans Frontières, and after the auction, which raised a total of $9.1 million, he said that he had only bought some of the items in the sale over the last few years, often at one-quarter of the price they had just realised. It was a further example of the huge prices now being paid for the very best material, a boom that was reflected in the art market and was driven by the influx of new money from Russia and the Far East. I liked what I had read about Gross a great deal. I admired his collection and his generosity, but I also appreciated his story, which was like mine on a grander scale. He had collected as a boy, given it up for real life, and then took it up again in his late forties as a way 'to reconnect with my childhood'. He was clearly a canny investor, and the person who appears to have taught him most was his mother. She taught him what not to do. She had bought mint sheets from the post office in the misguided hope that they would increase in value, just as I had done when I was young. But the stamps his mother gave Bill Gross were, even after several years, hardly worth face value. So now he invested in great rarity, and almost every major purchase he made was paying off.

I was fascinated by the sale of the Penny Blacks. Even a reproduction of the blocks in the catalogue displayed a richness and softness that summoned me back to the Dickensian post office, and I could see the haircut of the postmaster and his scissors slicing the sheet, and I wanted to rub my index finger over the chalky surface. Old stamps, especially line-engraved, have the power to transport the collector to a place in their childhood and far beyond; we remember where we were when we first saw a Penny Black and learnt of its lore from our fathers or at school, and even if we soon acquire a cheap one with poor margins and a heavy cancellation, and look at it for a lifetime, the appeal never lessens and the link with the beginning of our hobby is permanent. I have a Penny Black bought for £23 in 1976 in a small wallet-size album covered with fake green alligator-style vinyl. It is not a beautiful stamp, is not worth dramatically more than when I bought it, but it links me with a past that links all stamp people. (I have a pair of Twopenny Blues as well, finer examples and just as old and worth more, but they don't sing in the same way.) I never felt a strong sense of community with other collectors. Some form lifelong friendships at stamp clubs and monthly societies, but I was always terrified of revealing myself and being exposed; enthusiasm would probably have pulled me through, but everyone at these places seemed far older than me and their hair had oil and multiple partings, and I felt older just by looking at the list of names of honorary members, the Thwaites, the Festidges, the Belfrages. But for me the Penny Black was club membership at the highest level. Whatever else was happening around me – the family disintegrations, pressures of exams and then work, romantic complications – here was a comforting and reliable constant. It was flat, stowable, secret. Stamps seldom disappointed and never left you. My first meagre Penny Black is the only one I want from that time. I had never had the strong urge to buy a better one, or to expand to the later high-values (not that I could have afforded to). I have a particular love for the Jubilee set issued between 1887 and 1900, an explosion of colour and elaboration in carmine, rose, purple, green, scarlet, yellow and vermilion. But the feeling I get when I examine my Penny Black with its heavy black Maltese Cross cancellation is something that runs sideways through my veins, fizzing off the lining. It has something to do with being first – the first adhesive stamp issued, the first famous stamp in my album, one of the first of those great British inventions that would soon be thought useful throughout the world, like gas masks or the internal combustion engine. I felt proud when I saw that block of twenty-four go for $1 million in America. But goodness knows what Rowland Hill would have felt.

And just when I was considering the possibility of moving from errors into line-engraved Victorian, I received an email from Mark Brandon suggesting I should think again. It was not a personal email, but it seemed to be speaking directly to me. 'Dear Collector,' it began,

We have recently purchased in its entirety the world-renowned 'Jalapa Collection' of modern British Errors. This collection is basically COMPLETE to include all known missing colour and imperforate errors up to the year 2000 and was formed, with the help of ourselves, by an old client and friend over the past forty or so years.

Due to the vast scale of the holding we shall be gradually adding gems from this sensational collection over the forthcoming months to our website (first selection just uploaded under new items) and we invite you to view these at http://www.stamperrors.com.

We will, of course, have the entire holding at Stampex in February and invite clients to come and view these at our booth. In the meantime, please advise us of any specific 'wants' for that elusive error.

Kind regards,

Mark Brandon

This was a sensation, because as Mark Brandon wrote, the collection is basically COMPLETE! There was one stamp I had to have.

I wrote back immediately.

Hi Mark,

How exciting!

I'm still in the market for the Parliamentary Conference 1s 3d missing blue if you want to quote me a price on it . . . (presumably it's in a strip?).

Would love to find out more about Jalapa's collecting stories. Would you ask him if he'd be willing to talk now that he's sold?

Hope all's well with you. I'm going to see your father again at the end of this week . . .

Best,
Simon

At 8.31 the following day:

Hi Simon,
Great to hear from you.

Although the collection is virtually complete it, sadly, does not contain the Parliamentary strip . . . I did have one a few years ago but I managed to persuade the owner to part with it so that I could sell it on to another client.

I will certainly ask him if he would be prepared to share his collecting stories with you, please leave this one with me.

All the very best,
Mark

Almost Blue

In 2000, at a dinner to honour the Chelsea FA Cup-winning team of 1970, held at a Top London Hotel, I sat next to a man from the Franklin Mint who told me about the heirlooms to be treasured by your children and your children's children. Most of this crap was rolling off production lines in China: Victorian dolls, special editions of Monopoly and Scrabble, *Coronation Street* plates. My dinner companion was an honest man: he told me that they could be enjoyed by their recipients, but they could not be relied upon to increase in value. In fact, the opposite would most certainly be true, and as soon as they were removed from their packaging they would be worth only irony dollars. 'Someone actually bought this when it was new!' you could say as you spotted it at kitsch.com years later. 'I must add it to my collection.'

When the Chelsea dinner was over I went around the top table collecting autographs from Peter Bonetti ('Could you sign it Peter "The Cat" Bonetti?' I asked him. 'I'll sign it anything you like,' he said), John Dempsey, Marvin Hinton, Chopper Harris and Peter Osgood. Alan Hudson was due to be there too, but he had just been run over. They wrote their names on my photo of the triumphant team posing with the FA Cup, and a week later I had it framed and hung it on the wall outside my office. I thought it was a collectable. When Peter Osgood died five years later it became even more of one.

The photo hangs a few feet away from two large dark-blue cabinets containing about six hundred Chelsea lapel badges. These are made of scrap metal and coloured enamel, and it is clearly a collection that has got out of hand. I had a few in a box from when I used to go to Chelsea with my father, and I bought a few at the first big games I went to with my own children, and then something suddenly kicked in and we were buying everything we could from the stands outside the ground and collectors' fairs and eBay. Many badges featured individual players: 'Chopper Bites Yer Legs'; 'Osgood Is Good.'

Had he died a few years before, Peter Osgood's death would have made him eligible, indeed likely, to appear on a stamp. Up until the end of the twentieth century there was a formal understanding that, with the exception of royalty, no living person could be remembered in this way. It was seen as disrespectful, and possibly confusing; because stamps were traditionally linked with commemoration and anniversaries, the public might assume a person was dead just because they appeared on one. After the war there was mild clamour for Churchill to appear on a stamp, but the governmental postal committee decided that it was best to wait until he was dead.

Occasionally, there were errors. Roger Taylor, drummer with Queen, appeared in the background of a stamp celebrating the life of Freddie Mercury, who had died a few years earlier. There were letters of disquiet from smart Alecs in the philatelic press, but no one else seemed to mind, and shortly afterwards the rules were relaxed. These days anyone can appear on a stamp so long as they are commercial enough. So we have had half the English cricket team celebrating the Ashes, and at the beginning of 2007 we had the Beatles, including surviving members Paul and Ringo, being issued in eight different ways, and proving the most popular stamps the Royal Mail has printed apart from commemoratives with royals.

John Lennon would have been pleased: he was a stamp collector when he was young. In fact, his album, a green 'Mercury', suggests his schoolboy collection was almost as poor and erratic as mine. On 145 pages there were scattergun accumulations of GB, as well as India, Australia and Canada, places he would have had no realistic expectation of visiting, not least as a demigod. Or perhaps there were already vague intimations: he had practised his signature on several pages. There was also his address: 251 Menlove Avenue, Woolton, Liverpool. The album is worth rather more than mine. When it came up for sale in May 2005 at Fraser's Autographs (a sister company to Stanley Gibbons), it was described as 'a wonderful item . . . in very good condition, with scattered light toning and soiling to the signed page, worn but intact front cover spine and expected age and handling wear from a stamp collector'. When it was put on show to prospective purchasers, it was pointed out that even at an early age, Lennon was 'displaying a love of drawing'. He had demonstrated this by drawing a beard on stamps with the King and a moustache on the Queen. What was not mentioned was the fact that some of the stamps appeared to be attached to the album with heavy glue. The stamps on their own were worth about £3, but the album's provenance ensured an asking price of £29,950.

Freddie Mercury also collected when he was still Farrokh Bulsara in India. He was keenest between the ages of nine and twelve, with a particular interest in Great Britain, Aden, Monaco and Zanzibar, his birthplace. His collecting level can best be described as 'artistic', for he collected on unusual black album pages and designed his displays with great care for symmetry and colour. On one page he had used GB stamps to spell out the letter 'F'. He lost interest long before he became famous, but his album was looked after by his father, himself a keen collector of Zanzibar fiscals (government tax stamps).* Two years after Freddie Mercury's death in 1991, his father put both his own and his son's collections up for auction at Sotheby's.

His son's lot raised £3,320 plus VAT plus commission, purchased by the Royal Mail for the National Postal Museum. The album was then exhibited, and young philatelists and Queen fans were encouraged to do something they had not been allowed to do to any stamp album before: touch it. In fact, they received a certificate stating they had both viewed and touched the Mercury album, and *Stamp Magazine* reported that 825 people had received certificates during 1994. After the National Postal Museum closed down in 1998, Mercury's album went on tour to the World Philatelic Exhibition in Melbourne, where it was displayed in the Court of Honour and reportedly seen by more people than pages from the collection owned by the Queen.

For a while I made a habit of asking famous people I interviewed if they collected stamps.

Madonna: 'No! What makes you ask?'

John Terry: 'Stamps, no.' His thing was watches: 'This is a Rolex Daytona,' he said as he flashed his wrist. 'For winning the league I treated myself to a Franck Muller.'

Pete Townshend: 'I did collect stamps, yes, until I was about twelve, I think. Not brilliantly well, but I loved doing it.'

---

* A regular joke at auction houses is that it is always smart to collect Zanzibar, because as the auction catalogues are arranged in alphabetical order, everyone would have spent their money or gone to sleep by the time Zanzibar came around.

Not brilliantly well: this is how I would rate my own early philatelic health. I have one large cardboard box that once contained clementines from Spain and now houses all my philatelic passions from the ages of six to eighteen. It begins with torn stamps in the Stanley Gibbons Gay Venture album and ends with entire mint sheets preserved between stiff card, and in between is a sample of almost every collecting fad and gimmick the Royal Mail issued. Once I hoped these would have future value; now I wonder at my naivety and endless enthusiasm for gutter pairs, traffic-light blocks, miniature sheets, first-day covers, presentation packs, PHQ cards, booklets, year packs and exhibition souvenirs. I was grabbing at everything, the way one does when one is amassing rather than collecting, the way one hoards without knowledge. The Royal Mail marketing team absolutely adored me.

There are many written guides on how to collect stamps, some more patronising than others. My favourite was published in 1926 by C. F. Dendy Marshall, a Fellow of the Royal Philatelic Society and then owner of a valuable collection of early Victorian issues, including many proofs and essays. 'The first desideratum of a collection is that it should be more than a mere accumulation,' Dendy Marshall instructs. 'If the purse permits, and opportunity offers, it should commence with essays, proofs, documents &c. A frontispiece, not necessarily philatelic, may be quite an attraction, if well chosen, such as, for Great Britain, an engraving of the Wyon Guildhall medal.' Later on, Dendy Marshall advises: 'There are two practices, formerly more common than at present, which have done an immense amount of harm, and cannot be too strongly condemned. One consists of tearing off the margins of unused stamps which were at the edge of the sheet, the other of soaking or steaming used stamps off the paper.' The loss of margins reduced value and the ability to imagine the stamp on the original sheet, while the soaking and steaming often damaged the stamp and reduced evidence of postmarks.

'The next important question that arises relates to the number of stamps that are required, which of course depends on the extent to which variation is to be recognised. Many collections contain numbers of stamps which are really nothing but duplicates of one another, especially if the owner is well off, in which case the temptation to accumulate rarities is often apparently irresistible.' Dendy Marshall railed against collecting stamps in larger multiples than a strip of three or a block of four, complaining of how 'the power of a long purse' may deprive other collectors. His last pointer concerned the selection of album. In 1926 he found it useful to have his handmade in large oblong form, one hundred sheets to the album. Do not put too many sheets into one album, he warned, for the stamps will get rubbed.

My first album is in a terrible state. It barely has a cover, let alone a frontispiece, and there are far too many sheets in it, some of them empty, some of them so full that there is not a sign of yellowing album page. Stamps are piled on top of each other. All the stamps have been separated from their margins and soaked off their original backing. Some of them have, alarmingly, been glued in (I can't believe I did this myself, but who else would have had the chance?). There are stamps from places no one I know has ever visited, originating in sample packs from WHSmith or from charity appeals described in magazine adverts as 'missionary sacks'. The rest of my stamp box contains large quantities of duplicates and much futility. There are entire sheets of the 3 $^{1}/_{2}$p value from the 1973 wedding of Princess Anne to Mark Phillips, and a half-sheet from the 1974 of the 10p British Trees Horse Chestnut. There are albums of first-day covers addressed in my terrible teenage handwriting, many 'presentation packs' (the stamps issued in a plastic envelope with information about their history and design) and 'PHQ' postcards (official Post Office enlargements) of stamps celebrating Sailing and European Architectural Heritage Year (1975). There are also cigar boxes with small collections of marbles and sew-on patches with slogans such as 'Britain is Best', 'Keep on Truckin' and 'Just One Stroke'.

Most collectors do not just collect one thing. The core collection, whatever it is, is usually the symptom of a far more chronic malaise. The sickness spreads itself throughout a life like a shattered windscreen, and before one realises there are clusters of things all over.

A few years ago I began to seek out other people who collected, and to talk to staff at auction houses, who collected people who collected. This began modestly by talking to those who collected and sold rock and pop memorabilia. This was a relatively new pursuit, and it was the classic example of collecting without being aware of it. There is only a short step from owning a pile of records and CDs that you bought in a shop to actively seeking out rare recordings by a favoured artist or test pressings and acetates. The collectors' market for records gathered pace in the 1970s with picture sleeves and coloured vinyl; record companies realised what the Royal Mail had realised years before – that if you printed the same thing in multiple editions (for miniature sheets and booklets read coloured vinyl and 12-inch remixes), the smitten would buy duplicates.

The reason John Lennon's stamp album could be offered for £30,000 was because it contained several signatures, and Beatles signatures were the consistently hot item at the pop culture auctions. A good set that sold for £250 in the early 1980s went for £3,000 twenty years later. Many of these were hot in another sense, and Hillary Kay from Sotheby's and the *Antiques Roadshow* told me that before they can auction another signed copy of the White Album the item is sent to a man in Florida who can tell with a glance whether the autographs are 'good' or not, much like David Brandon with stamps. 'He will say, "Lennon and Ringo are good, but the others are wrong," or, "Only Paul's is really Paul, all the others are done by a secretary or machine." '

After rock memorabilia I started meeting people who collected famous sporting items – programmes, medals, trophies, match-worn shirts. This too is a fairly new area for the bigger auction houses, boosted by two things: the desire of older well-known sportsmen to handle debt and old taxes by selling their career highlights, and fans who once dreamed of emulating their heroes now finding they can bid for their trophies; they are not only buying reflected glory – sportsmen with mementoes won with the utmost endeavour selling to City boys with the utmost Christmas bonus – but also part of their youth.

I came across a man called David Convery in a crowded vault at Christie's in New Bond Street, and wherever he stepped he was surrounded by collectible items from upcoming sales. There were football objects in cardboard boxes next to tennis rackets and signed boxing gloves, and these were not far from German teddy bears and Beatles wigs and a Corgi James Bond gold Aston Martin DB5 in near-mint box with fully working ejector seat. It was hard to decide whether these collections were a priceless part of our cultural heritage or melancholy junk, or both, but it was clear that something new was happening to the value of our souvenirs.

Convery was a Scot with the sort of robust frame unsuited to most sports except fishing and darts. I met him when he was in his early thirties, and during his short adult life he has seen something interesting happen to the market in football memorabilia. In the summer of 1989 he was working in the Scottish Art department at Christie's Glasgow branch when it was decided to hold a specialist football sale. This was the first time a major auction house had attempted such a thing; annual auctions of cricket and golfing items were popular, but they dealt mostly with pre-war items and the buyers were a small band of well-heeled men with an obsessive interest in Scottish links and the 'bodyline' Ashes series. Football medals and old programmes were occasionally tacked on to these sales, or featured in general auctions, but the thought of a dedicated sale was often regarded as too working-class to attract sufficient funds. In the first auction, the gems included an 1897–8 England v. Scotland cap awarded to Ernest Needham of Sheffield United (which went for £620) and the football used in the 1903 Scottish Cup final (£480). There was also a lot of attic stuff – wooden rattles, faded photographs – and it all helped to push the total to £45,179. A year later, the next sale in Glasgow made £48,873. But in 1991, as news of the new market spread to players and collectors, the total came to £126,730. Fourteen years later, the sale of one item – the second FA Cup, used between 1896 and 1910 – was sold for almost four times that total, for £488,000.

In the basement, Convery pointed out a cardboard box containing a rare football shirt. He let me take it out, unfold it, and pose with it as he took my photograph; it was the shirt worn by Pelé in the 1970 World Cup final in Mexico. In fact, it was probably one of three shirts worn by Pelé in that match. He had one at the start of the game, almost certainly changed at half-time because of the heat, and then wore yet another when he went up to get his winner's medal. I was holding the second shirt.

Its value was uncertain, as few comparable items had come

up for auction before. In September 2000, the shirt Geoff Hurst had worn in the 1966 final went for £80,000, but that was considered to be a freak result: the hat-trick shirt, a feat never equalled. Pelé's jersey – yellow with green trim, number 10, still mud-stained – was worn in one of the greatest finals ever held, by the greatest player the world had ever seen. He scored the first goal in Brazil's 4–1 victory over Italy, a triumph that displayed such unfettered artistry that the memory of it makes mature people tearful. At the end of the match, half the defeated Italian team displayed one unexpected character trait: not despair, but ambition – they all wanted Pelé's shirt. Roberto Rosato, the defender, got to it first, and owned it for thirty-one years. And then in November 2006 a Christie's employee received an email from Rosato's daughter. Carola Rosato explained that her father's English wasn't so good, and she was making an enquiry on his behalf: would they be interested in selling the Pelé shirt? The first thought at the auction house was scepticism; perhaps it was a wind-up; perhaps the shirt was a fake. Carola Rosato then emailed some detailed photographs, and Christie's began to get excited. 'The key details gave it away,' David Convery told me. 'The badge, the stitching, the label – "Umbro World Cup Choice – Made in England".'

Convery did some further research, met Rosato in England, and became convinced that he had the genuine article. He decided on an estimate of £30,000–£50,000, and resolved to put it on the cover of the next catalogue. The key was the provenance; a bidder's mind would be put at rest that this really was the shirt Pelé had worn for the second half of the game (Convery estimated that the third shirt he wore – because he didn't want to pick up his medal half-naked – would be worth only a few thousand). But the true value of the shirt lay in its story, the yarn that linked it beyond fame to history. As with the Blue

Mauritius, worth lay in the ability to say who touched it first and where it had been. We like to feel we are in touch with our past, and that we may for a while control its future.

On Roberto Rosato's big day, the main attraction was displayed on a mannequin in a tall glass case to the auctioneer's right, but was removed from its cabinet at about 11.40. 'Thank you, Ladies and Gentlemen, coming to lot 114 now, Pelé's 1970 World Cup shirt, and I will open the bidding at £20,000. Thank you, 22,000, 25,000, 28,000, on my left here, 30,000 . . .' And so it went, swiftly reaching £75,000. At £80,000 there was a slight lull, but then a man standing at the back of the hall began taking on a buyer on the phone. The bid rose to £120,000, then £140,000. It helped that the auction was taking place in the same year as the World Cup in Japan and South Korea, boosting Asian soccer fever. 'Are you all done?' the auctioneer asked. '£140,000. Selling on the telephone at £140,000. Fair warning.' The hall drew a collective breath as the gavel descended, and many scribbled the sum in their catalogues, thus spoiling their resale value in future auctions. With commission, the total would come to £157,000, the highest price ever paid for a football shirt.

Outside the saleroom, a member of Christie's staff who spoke Italian called Rosato on his cellphone. Rosato was more than pleased. He kept asking, 'Are you sure?'

The buyer said he wished to remain anonymous – the buyer could have been a she, but not *really* – so we do not know whether the Pelé shirt was part of a collection that also included shirts by worn by Puskas, Eusebio and Maradona, or whether it was a one-off. But if it was a one-off, I find it hard to see how the purchaser would have been happy with that. I feel sure he is a collector now, bitten by something great and eager for more.

*

To make me feel a little bit better – a bit saner – about my desire for stamps, I began to hunt down people who collected things that were stranger. I read about a man called Ken Tye who collected light bulbs. Tye was writing a history of early incandescent light, and he considered himself the leading collector in Britain. He had about fifteen hundred bulbs and, the nature of this strange and fragile passion aside, seemed to be fairly normal. He did, for instance, often light up his bulbs to admire their beauty; others would regard this as sacrilege, just as collectors of rare records would never dream of actually playing them. But Tye loved the varying glows from the different filaments – the carbonised vegetable material that appeared in Edison's day at the end of the nineteenth century, the tantalum drawn wire and then tungsten that characterised bulbs from the early twentieth century. Tye wore quite large smoked glasses and had a round balding head, and he looked like he was turning into a light bulb himself, the way owners come to resemble their pets. I'd like to think this was a common trait – the collectors of Bernard Leach pottery soon looking brown and earthy, and collectors of antiquarian books appearing dank and troubled by their spines.

Certainly when I met a man called Lucifer in rural Sussex in 2006, he did look like someone who used to consume considerable amounts of acid. Lucifer was in his early thirties and collected blotting paper. Not the sort of blotting paper favoured by Dickensian scribes, but the sort used by the manufacturers of LSD in the last three decades or so to get their product to the market. More precisely he is a collector and designer of blotter art, and a former user of the molecules they were designed to contain. These days his collection is entirely clean and artistic, and it is a beautiful thing.

Lucifer told me that before LSD was made illegal in the mid-1960s, psychoanalysts and recreationists could get their drugs in several ways. Large pills were popular, as were infused sugar cubes. After proscription, the length of a jail term for possession was based on the weight of the LSD delivery method, and so the smart set looked for lighter ways to distribute their hits. Gelatin was tried for a while, but nothing proved as popular as thin absorbent paper; the acid could be dropped onto marked portions dose by dose, or an entire sheet could be dipped and then broken up.

Even users without heightened powers of perception soon began to notice that their individual hits had little logos on them. Pyramids and shields were popular at first, and then cartoon characters and strawberries. These motifs served a dual purpose: they signified the strength of dose, and they signified the doser. It was branding for hippies: proud LSD labs wished to establish their credentials as drug-makers you could trust. The early sheets of blotting paper were torn freestyle, but soon perforations ensured a better split and equality of high. By the late 1960s, some sheets of blotter art only began to make sense when seen as a whole design – a novel counter-culture art-form that lost its integrity as soon as someone tore a bit off and put it in their mouth.

Lucifer told me that Lucifer was his birth name and he didn't much trust surnames. When I arrived at his house, which he shared with three other creatives, one of whom was his girl-friend Twinkle, the first question he asked me was whether I'd like some chocolate. This turned out not to be Cadbury's, but a home-made brick kept in the fridge that contained cocoa beans from jungles and rare fruits and spices and something else. I had visions of never finding my way home. I had a small piece, and it was strong and delicious. He told me that an overnight guest was once staying with him who raided the fridge in the middle of the night and ate large amounts of this special chocolate and it took her one day to remember who she was and one week to recover.

Lucifer used to be a road traveller, but is now predominantly a spiritual traveller. He is also an eBay trader, and has sold many famous designs of blotter art and some of his own. He told me that his interest began in the second summer of love in the late 1980s, and since then he had amassed a varied and valuable collection. As Twinkle brought us tea with twigs in it, he showed me three albums' worth of historical images, each perforated into 900 or 1,000 squares. Obviously they reminded me of small sheets of stamps, albeit the sort that could mail you to another universe.

'The first sheet I saw complete was this Timothy Leary Profile,' he said as he unsheathed a highly complex multi-coloured design incorporating many visual interpretations of the teachings of the pro-LSD psychology professor. 'It has the skull and crossbones on his shoulder and musical notes coming out of his ear. It has the SMILE theory in the background – Space Migration equals Intelligent Life Extension. I think it was 1995, and I was at a rave site before the rave had started. There was a sofa around a fire, and I sat on that and someone turned up with a new sheet that had just been dipped and it was this one. People held it and went, "Wow!" You could feel the energy from it through your fingertips.'

In those days, each tab cost Lucifer between 50p and £3.50, depending on market forces and strength. He remembers that certain parts of certain sheets were stronger than others. Sometimes they were held up by a top corner after the dipping, so that the LSD would drip to the bottom or a corner. 'On the Timothy Leary I was told that the sheet was dipped again just on the skull and crossbones.'

Lucifer drifted into the rave scene from skateboarding and

high-adrenaline sports, but stopped using LSD in his early twenties. 'I felt that it wasn't safe enough. Every person that touches a dipped sheet adds their energy to it. I had taken various ones that had led me to negative perceptions. Not really a bad trip as such, but I had believed that the whole point was to reach some awakening or bliss, and I was missing that when I received heavy hallucinations and strange sounds. I was almost experiencing someone else's life history.' By then he had already begun to think that his future in the blotter art scene lay not as a consumer but as a creator and collector. 'This is *The Simpsons*,' he said as he flicked through his plastic folders. A well-thumbed and underlined copy of Aldous Huxley's *The Doors of Perception/Heaven and Hell* lay by the cushions on which we sat. 'And this is a *Beavis and Butt-head*, and the *Hendrix*, and *Easy Rider*, and the *Dancing Skeletons*. And the famous *Alice through the Looking Glass*, which is double-sided.'

He gave me one of his own designs, an intense mixture of symbols representing ancient tribal beliefs, Kabbalistic languages and swirling celestial bodies. I told him I collected stamps, which also had perforations, so there was a neat link there, and his eyes drifted away. He was too polite to say it, but I sensed his meaning was, '*Now* who's the strange one?' The printing of his blotter art was complex, he explained. 'There are 147 separate layers to enhance the clarity. I send them on a disc to someone in England, and then when this person has enough designs he books a ticket to America, goes over for the weekend, waits to see them printed, and then comes back with fifty copies of each design. I'm not sure where he goes in America. There are certain bits of information I'm happy not knowing.'

Lucifer acknowledges a certain risk attached to his calling.

'People can get rather alarmed if they just see all these sheets lying around. The police use a UV lamp – it will glow if LSD is present, and the lamp will also destroy it. But if you're a collector it's best to have them framed on the wall.' He has recently begun to sell blotters on the website he runs with friends called Hunab Ku (www.hunabku.biz). This site, which emerged from a shop in Glastonbury, has been some time in the making, but since fixing 'the time dilation components there is less chaotic flux emanating from the crystalline source'.

Lucifer is fairly new to the game. His enthusiasms run counter to the popular belief that the collecting generation is ageing and not being replaced. He speaks with awe of fellow designers and collectors Rick Sinnett, Alex Grey and James Clements, but in particular he admires the work of Mark McCloud, the creator of the *Alice* blotter and many more. McCloud, who lives in San Francisco and has been busted and acquitted twice for his suspicious-looking hobby, runs what he calls the Institute of Illegal Images. This is by far the largest blotter art collection in the world, with many unique items surviving not as sheets but only as single tabs. McCloud now sells art-print enlargements of the more iconic images for $1,000 each, including *The Mighty Quinn* (an Eskimo looking out to sea), *The Sorcerer's Apprentice* (thought to have been dosed with LSD from Albert Hofmann's own laboratory), *Snoopy* (featuring the dog in shades with what McCloud has described as 'an illegal smile'), and *Gorbachev* ('This is the Gorby that brought the Berlin Wall down!').

McCloud is blotter art's archivist, but there has yet to be an official catalogue establishing rarity and pricing structure, and the collecting market has yet to be tested by a major auction house. As with all valuable artefacts, there is also an emerging and convincing line in forgeries. Lucifer said there were about twenty serious collectors in the UK, but he was concerned that not all of them knew how to spot a genuine *Dancing Skeletons* from an impostor.

Not so long ago we seemed to be content to collect the things that made sense, the things that were in the game What Am I Bid? I once played with my dad. The Chippendale chair, the Sheraton bureau, the Ming vase, the Meissen dog. The things they had in common were that they were beautiful, useful or both. It's unlikely that the people from the Tang dynasty argued over whether their work was 'a design classic', or even whether their efforts would one day be collected. But now we seem to collect anything, or claim that two or more of anything is a collection. I tried to think what was the most absurd thing one could collect with deliberation and passion, beyond offspring or money. Butterflies, the first-day covers of the Edwardians; fossils, the Victorian craze; and before then tulips, the madness for which sprung up in the first half of the seventeenth century in the Netherlands and was later mirrored in the orchid mania of the 1980s – these were fads that had a certain logic to them, based either on ephemera or permanence, and upon our appreciation of beauty and diversity. The great naturalists collected specimens to prove their points.

But now we prove nothing beyond our ability to amass things and press 'Buy It Now' on eBay.

And yet, collecting anything makes sense to me. Ten years ago I would have scoffed at people who collected luggage tags, or at least not given them another thought. But now I embrace collectors of car air fresheners and chocolate wrappers, and my impression of strangers or the recently deceased increases when I learn, for example, that Henry Moore's wife Irina was a voracious collector of matchboxes. I have joined the Ephemera Society, where I am one of the youngest members.

I appear in the *Ephemera Society Handbook* as a collector of Tube maps. The Ephemera Society is not interested in stamps, but in things which don't have much of an established market in the wider world, or at least the world beyond Ephemera Society events, often held in Russell Square hotels. These included airline sick bags, Victorian scraps, copies of *Parade* with rusted staples. The things laid out haphazardly on the trestle tables at the Society's biannual sales are mostly printed matter, and often it is only the fact that they were once printed at all that gives them currency. They were meant to inform and then to be thrown away, but some of them survived and are now worth a quid or two. Hotel napkins. Labels from wooden fruit crates.

But what of the non-printed material that we write ourselves as notes and lists? Someone called Yvette phoned – she'll call again tomorrow. Please water the plants while I'm away. A dozen eggs, Frosties, ketchup. And what if we decided to collect these shopping lists and derived pleasure from it? I used to believe that this would be the most absurd thing any collector could aspire to, almost beyond the bounds of comprehension, and then I met someone who collected shopping lists.

Chris Moulin, PhD, a neuropsychologist specialising in Alzheimer's at the University of Leeds, did not volunteer this information from the off. We had been talking for a while about experiments he had conducted that were designed to repair a person's ability to learn. Twenty minutes passed, and then, somewhat sheepishly, he admitted that he collected shopping lists in an album, and told me that his fascination began after he found a list on the floor of a memory clinic which read 'bin liners, memory clinic, lunch'. His favourite is a piece of paper from a supermarket with just one word on it: 'Oil'.

This is not unusual. Marilynn Gelfman Karp has written a large illustrated book about strange collecting passions (it has a terrible title: *In Flagrante Collecto*). According to the dust-jacket, Karp is Professor of Art in the Department of Art and Art Professions in the Steinhardt School at New York University, which is itself a valuable collection of the word 'Art'. Her book contains a small section on her own love of shopping lists, and these are catalogued as if they were Roman coins or Renaissance masterpieces: '1: Group of Shopping Lists, 1991–2004, ink on paper, $3^{1/2}$–4" high; 2. Group of shopping lists, 1987–2004, ink on paper $3^{1/2}$–$8^{1/2}$" high.' These include, on a variety of paper, some of it crumpled, the instructions not to forget 'tanning oil, juice boxes, bathing suit, tennis, bottled water, snack bags'; 'breast pads, shredded cheese, 8 pepper, choco'; 'screen $28^{1/2}$ x 50, latch top, gate latch, putty'; '5 anchovies, 2 jam, 1 olives'; 'bread, grapes, milk, dye hair, 4 roses'.

And shopping lists are nothing.* Some people collect the little slips of paper inserted with bought clothes and electronics to confirm quality control: 'This garment has been thoroughly inspected by Inspector No. 44'; 'Inspected by Sandra'; 'We hope you'll enjoy the comfort, wearability and quality of these shoes that I have inspected' – this last note signed simply '3'. In 'The Volcano Collector', Susan Sontag writes of a man known as 'Picture-mad'. 'As a child he collected coins, then automata, then musical instruments. Collecting expresses a free-floating desire that attaches and re-attaches itself – it is a succession of

---

* I once heard the wife of a friend of mine proclaim, as if there were no loftier calling, 'I collect Emma Bridgewater!' A bright and often spotty brand of pottery ware for the breakfast table and beyond, EB could occasionally be seen in *Elle Decoration* but never in *World of Interiors*. I suppose one can indeed collect things from the kitchen department at John Lewis, and after hearing of her quest for EB, I chastised myself for feeling elitist. If this woman derives pleasure from collecting EB, then why should I feel anything but delight for her? (The reason is: because she collects Emma Bridgewater.)

desires. The true collector is in the grip of not what is collected but of collecting.'

All this stuff. When I enter my house there is a long wall of London Underground maps on the wall. One wall will not contain them – they have spread onto the opposite wall and up the stairs, the oldest from 1902, twenty-eight framed examples of the perfect lesson in form and function, beautiful in their simplicity and colour. I don't know why I began my collection, but I have pursued it at transport and book fairs and map and Internet auctions, and I have derived the usual thrills of outbidding and being outbid, and narrowing down my wants list from Edward Johnston and MacDonald Gill designs to the first maps of Harry Beck, from the District and Central lines alone to the first unified maps of 1906, from the ones with old stations like Mark Lane and Post Office to the opening of the Jubilee extension to Stratford. Visitors seem to like them when they come to the house, and have used the latest one to get home.

In the sitting-room there is a glass case with Technicolor Corgi and Dinky cars from television shows and movies, and I'd be embarrassed by them if they weren't so attractive and exciting in their original cardboard boxes, if they weren't so complete with their *Man from U.N.C.L.E.* Waverly ring, *Avengers* poison-tipped umbrellas, their Batman exhaust missiles and James Bond ejector seats. Besides, there was nothing unusual about these models or the rest of the collection – just the normal Thunderbirds/Joe 90/Captain Scarlet/Yellow Submarine/Saint/Kojak/Monkeemobile spread – and there was nothing there that most other British men in their forties wouldn't also desire.

Upstairs there are the two cases of enamel Chelsea badges, and crates of rare Elvis Costello records, mostly from the late

1970s when his singles had different sleeves throughout Europe and the vinyl came with different B-sides and colours. I don't know why I wanted six different copies of 'Less Than Zero' and ten of 'Watching the Detectives', and I never play them and seldom look at them, but I am reassured by *Record Collector* magazine that my eccentricities are not unique (or even rare).

I did not tend to question my collecting habits, I just enjoyed them. I thought that one day I might put everything on display and have my own little museum for the appreciative. But nowadays there is no avoiding the conclusion that my collecting habits are tied up with the death of my father. I became keener as the size of my family declined. Within a few years in my late teens I lost several relatives – grandparents, an aunt, a cousin – and I began to wonder whether stamps were in some way compensating for a family. They are a solace, and a way of restoring order. They may suggest an element of control in a fateful world – everything in its place, just like the old days.

I'm with Sigmund Freud on this. My brief period of not collecting stamps ended not long after my father died, and I was mad about other things as well – Esso coins, old magazines, Tube tickets.* Freud began collecting seriously just after his father died in 1896, but he had been thinking clearly about collecting the year before. Freud collected fertility figures;

* With a friend I collected a ticket from every station on the Tube system, in the days when they were either hard cardboard or softer yellow card with a brown magnetic strip on the bottom. Many of these were gathered by asking the man at Golders Green station to delve into his wooden bin and give us used tickets, but the elusive ones could only be obtained by going to the station in question and buying them. Cockfosters and Southgate were both hard to get. We arranged the tickets on a large piece of card in the same shape as they appear on the map, and I think we sent it into *Blue Peter* in anticipation. It came back with nothing. It then went into my friend's garden shed, and after a few years his mother threw it away.

inevitably, collecting was about sex, or the lack of it. 'When an old maid keeps a dog or an old bachelor collects snuffboxes, the former is finding a substitute for her need for a companion in marriage and the latter for his need for – a multitude of conquests. Every collector is a substitute for a Don Juan Tenerio, and so too is the mountaineer, the sportsman, and such people. These are erotic equivalents.'*

But what happens when you flip? I think that most collectors at some point question the purpose of what they're doing. Is collecting futile? What am I trying to prove? Why am I spending all this money on things I don't need?

Certainly the art world has a handle on this. In 2000, the British artist Michael Landy decided he had enough of things, and the way we define ourselves by what we possess, so he destroyed them in an event in Oxford Street called Break Down. Everything he owned went. Two years later the same thing happened in America, when a twenty-nine-year-old man called John Freyer decided he needed some spare money and didn't really need anything he had collected in his life, and so he put everything on eBay. Everything, including sideburns and half-consumed jars of food. He believed, and rightly so, that someone would be collecting even the most absurd thing he had to offer.

When I met Freyer in New York he was promoting a book called *All My Life for Sale*. He had in fact already sold everything, and so all there was left to do was collect the experiences of each sale in a compelling picture book. He hadn't just sold his things, including an answering-machine tape and his two false front teeth (a childhood accident on a golf course), he had also

* Quoted in 'Mille e Tre: Freud and Collecting by John Forrester', in John Elsner and Roger Cardinal (eds), *The Cultures of Collecting*, Reaktion Books, 1994.

visited the people who had bought them. He had sold a brick to a bidder in London (cost of brick $3, cost of postage $35, but Freyer felt embarrassed and only charged $10), and his sideburns went for $19.50 to a man in Pittsburgh who later reported he was disillusioned with his purchase. I watched Freyer as he set up a slideshow at Makor, a Jewish community centre on the Upper West Side. He was only one participant on a six-person panel. The others were all people who had bought something from Freyer on eBay in the last year. There was a man who had bought a Stevie Wonder LP, a woman who had bought a US army chair, a female rock critic called Mary Huhn who had bought an old Hawaiian instrumental album, and there was Adam Cohen, a reporter on the *New York Times* who had written a book about eBay called *The Perfect Store* and had bought Freyer's fish-print shirt. Cohen said that Freyer now had an imitator in Australia who was selling her life on a site called AMLFS.com (she couldn't use the full allmylifeforsale domain name, because Freyer had already sold it to the University of Iowa Museum of Art for $1,165 after thirty-four bids).

How strange, I thought, as I learnt about the person who had bought his bag of Porky's BBQ Pork Skins. Were people now collecting because they were keen to be part of a consumerist art statement, or just for the madness of it, to build up a lot of one thing no one else cared about? In this way one could become unique, and put down a marker on the earth. But then I realised I had done something similar without knowing it, and I saw that the person who had collected the strangest thing of all was me.

For about six years, between the ages of six and twelve, I had collected fluff. Not fluff as in 'something that is superficial', or even fluff as in 'error of delivering lines on stage', but actual fluff from a green carpet in my house.

I don't know how this began, or even why I did it. I used to sit on the stairs in my childhood home and pick at the green carpet with my thumb and forefinger, gathering what I could until I had a thin strip of soft fibres about two inches long and an inch wide. I would then place this on my forehead between my eyebrow and my temple, and derive unqualified pleasure from it, especially when I fell asleep at night. After a few days I would tire of one particular shape or thickness of what I had come to call 'fluff', and then start the process again, keeping my old samples in a tin.

What more can I tell you about this, other than that it helped if you put a few drops of water on the carpet first to aid the tension between finger and weave? For a year or so I did this openly, and then my parents began to object to the unusual wear on certain parts of the carpet towards the top of the landing, and I was forbidden to pick fluff any more. My mother asked a department store for some small green carpet samples so that I could pick in my room without ruining the house, but these were a very poor substitute and usually wouldn't bind properly. I kept picking on the stairs for another five years, built up quite a collection, and then just as suddenly grew bored with it and stopped.

My stamp collecting, by comparison, was a reasonably respectable and basic thing to be getting on with. I was following a path laid down over decades – the natural, predictable and aesthetically pleasing way of accumulating anything interesting: one of every picture stamp and diverting oddities. But some people didn't collect like this, including an old friend of mine called Paul Hersh. I was aware that Paul had collected for years, but we had never talked about it. My wife was friendly with his wife, and his wife would occasionally worry that he was spending a bit too much time and money on stamps, but during my fallow period I never thought to question him about this. We spent our time together talking about his work producing comedy shows for the BBC.

But after I had become hooked on stamps again we got around to the topic immediately, and now we talk of nothing else. His collection is somewhat specialised. In fact, it is the most specialised and craziest collection I have ever seen. It is so specialised and so crazy that he asked me to change his real name when I wrote about it and him, for fear of ridicule from those who may not understand. Hersh collects stamps from Batum and also GRI overprints (*Georgius Rex Imperator*, George V being the reigning monarch at the time of overprinting), but his big thing is Machins. These stamps are the basic labels of postage that people in the UK use every day. They have the Queen's head and the denomination and that's it – no illustration commemorating a special event, just a single-colour background, a big profile of the Queen's crowned head and shoulders based on a bust by Arnold Machin, and the number 1p, 2p and upwards in a corner, or maybe the class indicator '1st' or '2nd'. (British stamps, being the first, have the honour of being the only ones not to bear the name of the issuing country.)

When I first went round to Paul Hersh's house and he took his Machin albums from the shelf, he said, 'Are you ready?' But I wasn't ready at all. Each page of each album had the same stamp on it. There were pages and pages of identical bright green, dull orange, blue, almost blue, and deep olive-grey stamps, not to mention the violet, carmine, ochre-brown and ultramarine.

'How many of these do you have?' I asked him, pointing to the bright-blue ones. 'About 150.'

'And how many Machins overall?' This took him a little longer to work out.

'About 3,360. There are about twenty or thirty I'm missing. But of course that's not including booklet panes and coils. So you could say I only do the fag-end of it.'

They were not, of course, all the same. In fact, they were all different, though you could only tell with the aid of a perforation counter, an ultraviolet lamp, and a ten-inch-thick two-volume catalogue with monthly updates. A 20p stamp has many variations of paper, printer, printing process, gum, phosphor band, shade, perforation, underprint, fluorescence and numerical design, and it takes a certain sort of individual to care. And if they do care, they will also be concerned about many other values, including the vaguely unimaginable $20^{1/2}$p.

The Machin first appeared in June 1967. Arnold Machin was a painstaking sculptor working on a profile of the Queen for new coinage when asked by Tony Benn to produce an image for the definitive stamp. This would replace the portrait produced from the photographic studio of Dorothy Wilding that had been used since her coronation and was looking dated, and the new design was intended to be flattering, regal and simple. It was also intended to last, which, with very modest alterations, it has done for more than forty years. At the beginning of 2008 it overtook the Penny Black and Twopence Blue as the longest-lasting stamp design in the world, undergoing some four hundred different basic colour or price variations (before Paul Hersh and his friends began finding other things interesting or wrong). The stamp has become one of those everyday icons that we use without thinking. Once we have looked at the value, only the most retentive collectors are able to match a stamp's colour to its price. It is estimated that the Machin has been printed almost 200 billion times.

The things that interest Hersh include the following facts and firsts: an early proof of the stamp was printed with the

Queen cut off at the neck, but she judged this too naked, approving the design only after the addition of a corsage.

The photograph of Arnold Machin's bas-relief sculpture of the Queen was taken in misty half-light in the car park of the printers Harrison & Sons so as best to define its shadows and details.*

The first three stamps – the 4d, 1s and 1s 9d – were printed with phosphor bands to aid automatic sorting, and were also the first stamps in Britain not to have a watermark (the coated paper and phosphor was regarded as guard enough against forgery).

The two-tier first- and second-class postal system was introduced in September 1968, with second class costing 4d and first class 5d. For a year after decimalisation was introduced on 15 February 1971, letters could be sent with a mixture of old and new stamps.

In 1985, for the first time since the Penny Black, the cost of postage went down, second class reduced from 13p to 12p.

In the mid-1980s there were serious attempts to find a replacement design for the Machin, and several straight-on portraits were essayed instead of the traditional image facing towards the left, but they were all rejected; it was tacitly acknowledged that the Machin would endure to the end of the Queen's reign – the older the monarch, the younger and more flattering our vision of her.

Paul Hersh was born in 1960, seven years before the first Machin was printed. He began collecting at the age of eight or

* Harrison & Sons Ltd is not the oldest stamp-printing firm, but in the UK it has been the most productive. In the sixteenth century, Richard Harrison was a Freeman of 'the mystery and art of printing', and the firm that carried his name held the virtual monopoly in British stamp-printing from 1934 to the 1980s. At one stage it was printing stamps for more than a hundred countries. It was bought by DLR in 1997 (later De La Rue Security Print).

nine, but it was mostly mint stamps from the post office and first-day covers. His grandfather bought him a few things, he joined the stamp club at school, and he stopped at about fourteen. He can't quite pinpoint why he got back into it, but he thinks the advent of the home computer was partly responsible. 'Stamps were made for computers,' he told me, 'because they look beautiful when scanned and enlarged, it's so easy to catalogue and trade them, and the nerdery of stamps and the early nerdery of computers were made for each other.'

Having spent many hours talking to Hersh about his stamps, I liked him even more than before. Looking at his albums made me feel very good, because I realised that there were people in a far worse philatelic state of health than I was. 'I got into this very gradually,' he said. 'I used to think there were perhaps six varieties of any one stamp, and when I discovered there were ten or twelve I thought it would be fun to get them all. Then you buy a detailed catalogue and you see there are twenty, so that extends the challenge. Then I found out about the Deegam Handbook [the ultimate guide to identifying and cataloguing all Machins, produced by the fanatical philatelist Douglas Myall], which lists absolutely everything and helps you identify them, and I saw that up until then I had only been dabbling. There are hundreds! It's cosmic! If I had foreseen how I was tumbling helplessly into it all then I would have shot myself.'

Heinz

In biology lessons I was taught that the big human limb joints worked like elaborate machines. The shoulder, elbow, knee and ankle, an intricate system of pulleys and weights and cogs and lubrications: when they worked you wouldn't think twice, but when they didn't you knew about it. One hot London afternoon in the early 1980s the left knee of my uncle Heinz stopped working, and as we walked across Regent's Park every animal in London Zoo surely realised something was wrong. It was the noise: unhealthy, unnatural, unforgettable. It was as if a comedy oak door (creeeeaaaakkkk) had fallen on pine cones in the frost (crrruunnnchhh). The mechanism had gone. Heinz's lower leg was wooden, and some part of it – perhaps the attachment to what was left of his original leg – needed linseed or cod-liver oil and bedrest. Heinz's leg had been blown off at the end of the 1948 Israeli War of Independence, and if only I'd known it needed so much maintenance I'd never have set out on that walk, or at least made sure we didn't get lost. I learnt a lesson that day: modern wars are about oil, but for Heinz the peace was about oil too.

Heinz Bauernfreund (trans.: 'Friend of the Farmer') was married to my mother's sister Eva. My mother came from Israel to London to marry my dad, and Eva stayed in Israel to marry a soldier. They were a lovely couple, but not obviously well matched. Heinz was a dashing model of uprightness, and had a job for life in life insurance; Eva was more rotund and warm: *gemütlich*. They had handsome children, a very busy kitchen, and infidelity. And then there were stamps, which occupied most of Heinz's leisure time and none of Eva's, a gender divide fairly mirrored throughout the world. Some couples get used to it – embrace it even – and some never do, and for my aunt I think her husband's philatelic devotions presented another reason to cast her gaze elsewhere.

They lived in Zahala, a spacious manicured village northeast of Tel Aviv, and the first thing you noticed when you entered their home was how ordered everything was. More particularly, you noticed how irritable Heinz would get if a cushion or drinks coaster was moved beyond a Heinz-defined comfort zone, usually measured with a slide-rule. My father was a little bit like this, and I inherited the gene, but we had it mild next to Heinz. There was an extensive collection of miniature liquor bottles Heinz had picked up on his travels over the years, one hundred or so, some of them very old and definitely undrinkable. He had arranged them on a thin shelf that ran across the top of the door of the main reception room, one long limbless parade-ground. They were so high that guests would never be tempted to rearrange them. But occasionally the movement of the door below would jog a bottle a fraction of an inch out of line, and Heinz couldn't sit down until he had climbed up and set the miniature world to rights. What would Freud have diagnosed in those days before obsessive–compulsive disorder? A need for reassurance; the pleasure and security of ownership; a desire to have everything just as it was and should be forever.

Zahala was neat too. Built after the war for career soldiers and permanent casualties, it was like a model kibbutz without the early mornings. For years its most famous resident was General Moshe Dayan, the Israeli defence minister during the Six Day War. Dayan lost his left eye fighting in Lebanon in 1941, and he wore his black eye-patch like a medal of honour (his bodyguard sold it after his death, and it appeared on eBay to maximum outrage in 2005). When a drawing of Dayan appeared on a first-day cover, my uncle walked a few paces up the road and got him to sign it. Zahala's other famous resident was Ariel Sharon, a future prime minister, though few would have predicted it during my uncle's time. In the early 1970s, when I first saw him at the Zahala falafel stand during a holiday, he was a bullish military leader newly embarked on a political career, and people in the neighbourhood were still very conscious of his personal tragedies. Sharon's first wife died in a car crash in 1962, and five years later their eleven-year-old son Gur and a friend were playing with the family gun collection – as Israeli kids in Zahala used to do – when one of them went off. Sharon was at home for Rosh Hashanah, the Jewish New Year, and his son died in his arms. In the mourning and distress that followed, local mothers rounded up as many family guns as they could, and delivered them to Moshe Dayan's house.

Heinz also had a gun, and he didn't give it up. It was self-defence. My other Israeli uncle had a pistol too; the founding generation never felt secure within their borders, national or domestic. In Heinz's case the gun was also self-defence against anyone who might burst in and make a grab for his first-day covers.

He kept his stamps in a humidity-controlled cabinet in the coolest part of the house, which fortunately also happened to be his study. Or maybe he just designed things that way: he would happily endure sweltering summer nights in bed in the back room, so long as his stamps were cool and safe. But would they be safe even in the study?

I slept in the same room as his stamps for more than a month one summer when I was eighteen, and how Heinz's nerves held out I'll never understand. Of course the stamp cabinet was permanently locked (this wasn't really about trust; it was about common sense, and every collector would have done the same). But I still could have spilled something over the cabinet, or knocked into it, or created so much friction when masturbating beneath the sheets that the whole room would have caught fire. Heinz slept in the next room, or probably didn't; I'm sure he was up every night with his ear to the wall, listening for potential disaster.

Because of its particular history, Israel only began issuing stamps in its name 148 years after Britain. This created philatelic problems. Every Jew wanted those first stamps, philatelist or not, and many non-Jewish collectors wanted them too. What they lacked in beauty they made up for in symbolism. The first stamps were issued on 16 May 1948, two days after the proclamation of the state, but they had been printed secretly in the weeks before, in the last days of the British mandate; they do not bear the name Israel, but Doar Ivri (Hebrew Post). There was a similar nervousness about their design. They depicted ancient coins, from the three-pruta half-shekel from AD 70 showing a palm tree and fruit, to the 1,000-pruta silver shekel from AD 69 showing a ceremonial goblet. Each denomination was printed in one dull colour only, orange, green, red or brown, and they had stubby perforations; nothing really to get the heart pounding.

Hundreds queued up on a Sunday morning to buy the

stamps, and for the most part supply kept up with demand. The problem for the collector was, what was one actually collecting? New issues were fine, but if everyone had them, what could set your own collection apart? Where was the specialisation and pride and prospect of jealousy? With no rarity, these were merely historical souvenirs. But then something changed. The stamps were originally issued with 'tabs', white perforated pieces of paper attached to the stamp at the foot or side, and the tabs contained written information about the origin of the stamp or details of the illustration. On the first issue, the tabs carried a Hebrew translation of the inscriptions on the coins. On an issue later in the year there was information about Jewish festivals.

At the beginning, most collectors thought the tabs unwieldy and superfluous, and stripped them away before placing the stamps in their albums. Quite a large mistake. Some collectors argued that the tabs were integral to the design, and within a few years their views were accepted by all. If you had kept them attached you were already sitting on something quite valuable; and if you hadn't you cursed yourself. Heinz had kept the tabs. A man with a wooden leg knew the value of completeness. All he had to do now was keep them from sticking to his acid-free pages as the thermometer bubbled.

All the stamps Heinz sent to me in London had tabs; unfortunately he only started sending them over in the early 1970s, by which time no one removed them, and stamps with tabs were worth only face value. To me, they were worth less than face value. I never collected Israel, but by the time the regular packets of mint issues and first-day covers started coming over by airmail every two months I was too frightened to tell him. I felt I couldn't concentrate on more than one country, and I was barely able to keep up with the GB output, such was the ceaseless appearance of stamps celebrating roses and cyclists and prison reformers. The other problem was, I found the Israeli stamps boring. Rather than David Gentleman and other elegant designers, they had designers called O. Wallish and F. Krausz, and they were seldom blessed with visits from a muse. Many stamps seemed to rely on things that were originally big – paintings, buildings – that were then made smaller and smaller the way people did when photocopiers first came out. They weren't designed, they were miniaturised. Also, how many bird stamps can one country produce? You couldn't fault the free-spirited hope suggested by these flapping creatures, and they were certainly preferable to something celebrating the latest tank movements, but I found them flat and clumsy. The packages came through from Heinz and immediately disappeared into a box. I thanked him for them whenever I saw him, but I should have told him, as delicately as possible, to save his money.

I was going to tell him when he came to London in the early 1980s. It was a lovely day in early summer, and we thought perhaps a trip to the zoo. Heinz didn't really like domesticated animals, especially pets, particularly chickens. He never ate chicken, not even kosher chicken, and chicken in Israel is very popular. So obviously this became a standing joke before almost every meal.

'What are we eating today, Eva?' I'd only ask this when Heinz wasn't around. My aunt's eyes lit up with glee.

'Chicken!'

It never got any more or less funny. We couldn't actually say 'chicken' in his presence, because even the word would sometimes tip him over the edge (he did have a sense of humour, but not when it came to this). I never learnt why, assuming it must have been an early bloody experience. But animals in cages he quite enjoyed, especially monkeys. London Zoo had long abandoned its Chimps' Tea Party, but there was still plenty of bum-scratching and nit-picking and mindless screeching to be had in the monkey enclosure, so we made our way there via the scenic route from Primrose Hill.

This was not a complex journey. You didn't need satnav to walk over a hill and into the zoo entrance on the other side, but somehow I got confused with the Inner and Outer Circle, and went in the wrong direction. We were almost at Parkway in Camden Town when the first unhappy sounds began to emerge from his trousers.

Heinz didn't say anything, and at first I thought it might have been his shoes.

'Is everything all right?' I asked

'Fine.'

'Want to sit down?'

We did sit down for a bit on a bench, and I apologised for getting lost. But then we had to go on. There were no cabs. There were no mobile phones to call cabs. So we turned around, and the noise started up again, much louder than before. It now had an industrial air. I don't think it hurt him, but it didn't sound comfortable. We walked on, to the consternation of passers-by. The noise grew. This was at a time when there were still street traders outside the zoo – men with giant balloons, men who would place a slender loris on a child's shoulder and take photos with menaces – so perhaps people thought that Heinz was a new addition to the clan ('Roll up! See the Israeli with noisy trousers!'). But no one gave us money, and my embarrassment grew. For a long while it seemed we were doomed forever to walk the earth and never find peace. We didn't enter the zoo, but found a taxi at its entrance, and we were both sweating heavily as we climbed in. As we drove home, Heinz joked that he wanted to kick me with his false leg, but by now it was sounding like the Six Day War and the cabbie would have dived for cover.

Heinz and Eva died within a few years of each other, when I was in my thirties. I don't know what happened to his stamps. I assume he had given someone the keys to his cabinet when he had the chance, but perhaps not. Perhaps his son, once an army captain, had to break the wooden door open with a tool.

But I know what happened to the stamps he had sent me. There were two shoeboxes of them, predominantly first-day covers, all of them with tabs. I didn't know how valuable they were until I placed them on eBay in October 2006. I offered them as a job lot. 'Israel: Complete fdcs 1972–1983 and some mint sets.' I described what they were, the ceaseless parade of national pride. There were five bidders. The winning one, Henry3336, lived in Radlett, Hertfordshire. Along with his stamps I sent Henry a brief outline of their origin, but I didn't mention the zoo story. I put the £81.25 towards a night in a hotel in Oxford with my girlfriend.

Missing T

A stage version of *Chitty Chitty Bang Bang*, one of my favourite childhood films, opened at the London Palladium on 19 March 2002, my forty-second birthday, and to mark the occasion I took a train to Dundee to visit my first Technicolor sweetheart. Heather Ripley, who played Jemima Potts, was seven when the film opened in December 1968, and I was eight, and I saw no reason why she wasn't the girl for me. Thirty-five years later I went to find out if this was still true.

She was now forty-one. She opened the door of her terraced house near where she grew up in Broughty Ferry, on the outskirts of Dundee, overlooking the Tay. 'Hello Simon,' she said. 'I do hope you're not going to write horrible things about me.' She spoke with a strong Scottish accent but timid voice. In the front room there were many dramatic examples of what she called drift art, assemblages of wood and other debris that had come ashore to be made into mirrors and picture frames. This was one of her many interests, along with peace campaigning, website design and getting back to acting.

She told me she was an only child in a fairly affluent family. Her father and grandfather ran an ophthalmic optician's business in Dundee, and they spent summers in France and winters skiing. Her mother got a job as a wardrobe mistress at Dundee Rep, and Heather used to go after school to watch the rehearsals. 'I remember Macbeth in particular,' she said. 'My father made the head for the ending and stuck it on a pole at the bottom of my bed.'

She enjoyed hanging round the theatre, and one day fate intervened. The play *Roar Like a Dove* was one week from its opening when the young girl in the cast fell ill, and Heather took her place. The thing she remembers best was a scene in which she was given a glass of Coke, not something she was allowed at home. A talent scout saw one performance and sent a note to casting agents with the news that she was a confident performer who might be suitable for other things, one of which turned out to be a film currently casting in London.

Based on the book by Ian Fleming, *Chitty Chitty Bang Bang* was a junior James Bond with songs. The star car had all the gadgets: wings, inflatable rafts, rotating blades. There was a mad inventor, some German spies, prim love interest with a woman called Truly Scrumptious, and a grandpa who once shot an elephant in his pyjamas. It also had the most terrifying of nightmares, a Nazified childcatcher with a leery smile and the most crooked finger in movie history.

As a comic counterbalance, Dick Van Dyke reprised his famous English accent four years after *Mary Poppins*, and there were a few great set pieces – in a sweet factory (marauding dogs, James Robertson Justice) and a fairground (Arthur Mullard, Barbara Windsor). It also had two apple-cheeked children, Jemima and Jeremy Potts, who sang like doves and had perfect manners. No young boy worth his Corgi car would fail to fall for Jemima with her white pinafore and toothy smile. (Personally, I had just recovered from a phase of being jealous of Jack Wild in *Oliver!*)

Six months before filming began, Heather and her family went to London for a screen test. 'They thought I was perfect for the part, apart from the accent,' she remembered. 'But they said that wasn't a problem as they'd get rid of it. I thought that sounded a bit ominous. What did they mean? Brain surgery?'

The filming, at Pinewood and in France and Germany, took more than a year. The flying sequence was particularly exciting, filmed with the car high up on a tilting pole, and Dick Van Dyke was the source of endless japes. 'I didn't know for years that he was an alcoholic then.'

Her life changed when the film was released. 'My most vivid memory was of the photographers hanging out in the playground trying to get pictures of me. I found that really disturbing. And then my entire family was hassled. My father had had an affair while we were away. They were terrified of a huge scandal.'

Her schoolfriends would sing 'Chitty Chitty Bang Bang' at her.

'In a nice way or a horrid way?' I asked

'It's not really possible to sing "Chitty Chitty Bang Bang" in a nice way.'

My own life changed for the better when the film and its merchandise were released. It was the beginning of a passion not just for Jemima/Heather, but also for metal and plastic souvenirs on which she and her family and their car were portrayed. For me, this was the birth of tack, something I would later detest when my children reached Disney age. I had the lunchbox, the poster, the soundtrack, the sweets. These days it all seems a bit girly, but at the time I felt only a pride in ownership. I told Heather that I still had the Corgi model with the extending wings and the bejewelled headlights. I explained that I had lost all four of the tiny plastic figures, but had recently bought them on eBay. I feared they might have been replicas. I think she felt a little uncomfortable with the way this conversation was turning, as if I was about to bring out a scrapbook containing photos of her in the shower, and pictures of every man she ever met, with their eyes blacked in with Biro. Sensing her unease, I edged the talk away from my Corgi/Dinky collection of TV/film-related cars towards her post-Chitty years.

After her parents' divorce, Heather moved with her mother to a small village south of Dublin where her future stepfather managed a stately home. She took her stepfather's surname, and shunned any further involvement in the child-star business. Domestically, life wasn't like the movies at all. Or rather it wasn't like most movies, but it was a bit like *Chitty*: money was short, and her earnings from the film were held in trust until she was eighteen. After ten years of the money being invested, Heather told me she thought it was still only worth about £7,000.

She moved back to Dundee at fourteen and drifted down to London at the height of punk. She worked in hotels, failed to get acting work, and came back to Scotland to join the family eye business. In her early thirties she moved with her two young children to Findhorn, the alternative spiritual community in northern Scotland. There they were visited by one of the founders of Earth First, who brought videos of the anti-logging campaigns in Australia.

Soon she became a campaigner herself, first against road-building on the site of a prehistoric burial chamber on the northern line of the Callanish standing stones in Lewis, and then against the Newbury bypass. You can't escape the irony: the woman who once sang in the back of that beautiful thirsty car did 'as much sabotage as possible'. Her children joined in, cutting fences at night and generally making as much of a nuisance of themselves as they could. She said it was great.

By the time I met her, her campaigning was limited to weekends and emails (she sent me one after just giving money to 'an Irish Zen Buddhist monk who works with death-row prisoners in the States – he's eating out of dumpsters, awaiting heart surgery – got badly beaten up by police at a Free Mumia Abu-Jamal demo').

Her other main interest was *Chitty Chitty Bang Bang*. She was happy to receive an invitation to the musical at the Palladium, even if she did have to ask for it. She is no longer disturbed by her peculiar fame, and increasingly uses her birth name again, not least at fan conventions where she signs photos for £15. She is keen to write a book about her experiences, possibly with Adrian Hall, the boy who played Jeremy, now a drama teacher. 'If there's money to be made, why not?'

After several hours in her charming company – a chat at her house as her labradors played at her feet, a lavish Indian meal during which she sought out the most expensive item on the menu, every minute ticking by without me having the courage to tell her how much I fancied her then (no good way of saying it: if I fancied her *then* would she take this to mean I didn't fancy her now? Or would it suggest that I was coming on to her?) – I sent her an email asking what she hoped for her children and herself in the next ten years. She answered: 'World peace, justice and equal rights.' I thought: What a terrible cliché. But then I realised that this was just what she would have said as a seven year old, and who else did I know who had retained such pure dreams?

It was a long journey home. I had plenty of time to consider why I couldn't tell her how she was the subject of my fantasies almost forty years before. What is it that stops us saying these words? I promised myself that in future I would tell people how much I liked them now or in the past. It wasn't yet time for my loss-of-youth crisis, but I had begun to value things I had previously taken for granted. These were the obvious things: friends, comforts, securities.

And so when the chance came to meet Tasveer Shemza a few years later I was determined to tell her exactly how I felt.

Tasveer and I were six when our lives crossed. It was June 1966, the World Cup finals not yet under way. I was watching television, either a Monday or Thursday at five-ish, *Blue Peter*. John Noakes and Valerie Singleton – only two presenters then, outnumbered by their pets – were about to announce who had won the competition to design Britain's first Christmas stamps. I had just begun collecting, and I had the largest possible Caran d'Ache pack upstairs in my room, so I was sure I was in with a very good chance.

I had sent in a picture of a sort of snowman. There were about four and a half thousand entries in the competition, and probably four thousand of these were either snowmen or reindeer, but mine was unique. It was a drawing of a Snowqueen – a normal snowman with buttons for the bottom half, but in place of the smaller lump of snow on the top with the eyes and carrot-nose, I had stuck the Queen's head. It was a sensation, and quite possibly treasonable. I had sketched the Queen's profile from earlier stamps, painted it silver, and off it went to BBC Television Centre with a wave of certainty about it. And now it was judgement day, and I was ready for glory. A Snowqueen.

Tony Benn, the Postmaster-General, had launched the competition a few weeks before, one of his last jobs before joining the Cabinet as Minister of Technology. The PMG, as the job was known, did not have absolute power to decide on stamp issues – this was the responsibility of an uncomfortable triumvirate composed of the Queen, the PMG and the Post Office Stamp Advisory Committee, the last as crusty and sensitive as a knee scab – but Benn set about the task as if he did. Most of his predecessors in the post had been content to sit it out until something more exciting came along, and for the likes of Neville Chamberlain, Clement Attlee and John Stonehouse something did. The job had begun at the start of the sixteenth century when the King appointed Sir Brian Tuke to take responsibility for the security and topicality of his letters (the prototype for Next Day Special Delivery) and 460 years later it was subsumed within various departmental portfolios after the Post Office Act of 1969. But while Tony Benn was there, from 1964 to 1966, he made quite a noise, and his biggest bang came in 1965 when he tried to remove the Queen's head.

This wasn't a republican thing, he claimed, it was an artistic one, a desire to free up more space for creative expression. Benn, who was not a philatelist, had become friends with the graphic artist David Gentleman, the designer of several commemorative stamps of the early 1960s, and with Benn's encouragement Gentleman had come up with designs for stamps that incorporated the phrase 'UK Postage' in place of the Queen.

In his diary, Benn describes a trip to Buckingham Palace to discuss the issue. Part of his forty-minute audience was spent on his knees as he passed the Queen enlargements of stamps commemorating the Battle of Britain. The Queen, who has no need for stamps on her own letters, apparently perused them with interest. Benn mentioned that it was widely perceived that no stamps could be submitted to her if they did not contain her portrait, and he wondered aloud if this was something she was aware of (and wondered to himself if it could be changed). Benn said that the inclusion of her portrait, which had occupied between half and a quarter of commemorative issues (and almost the whole stamp on definitive – i.e. plain – ones), meant that the country's top miniaturist designers were terribly restricted in their output. Benn had just established a Fellowship in Minuscule Design to encourage more stamp art, and he had visions of stamps celebrating not only the Seventh Parliamentary Conference, but everything that was good in Britain: composers, landscapes, painters, architecture, birds and flowers. 'The Queen was clearly embarrassed and indicated that she had no personal feeling about it at all,' Benn recalled. 'I said I knew she wouldn't . . .'

Benn left the Palace elated; he had won a great victory for philately and British exports. 'Am now convinced that if you went to the Queen to get her consent to abolish the honours list altogether', Benn recorded later that day with great relish, 'she would nod and say she'd never been keen on it herself and felt sure the time had come to put an end to it. Of course when you do that you have to be terribly charming and nice, and I tried as hard as I could to do a little Disraeli on her with all the charm I could muster.'

Alas, he should have done the big Disraeli. The establishment wheels ground out their disapproval of his white-hot designs, and in the weeks that followed he received discouraging clues that his optimism was misjudged. When he asked to see the instructions sent to prospective illustrators of the stamps to mark the opening of the Post Office Tower, he found that no changes had been made to the wording at all. It still read, 'The Queen's head must be a dominant feature of the designs.' Then he received bad news from the Queen's private secretary and Harold Wilson. The Queen's head would have to stay, although it could be reduced to a cameo silhouette rather than a line-drawing, and thus become a less distracting and obtrusive part of the image. According to Benn, Wilson had his own theory about the volte-face: 'She is a nice woman,' Wilson told him, 'and you absolutely charmed her into saying yes when she didn't really mean it.' Wilson then went off to one of his regular audiences with the Queen, a meeting that lasted for an hour and quarter. Ten minutes were spent on the Rhodesian crisis, and one hour and five minutes on stamps.

Away from philately, this was quite a time to be PMG. Benn ushered in the system of all-number phone numbers, as opposed to MEA 3111 (for Meadway) or Ham 9797 (Hampstead). He also had meetings about extended sorting codes: the first – WC1 – to direct an item to a region, the next – 4DJ – to define the smaller area within that region. But mostly he was occupied with stamps.

In April 1966, Benn received a phone call from Devon. A man told him he had tried unsuccessfully to send out thirty important bills, but he was unable to get the required 3d stamps. He therefore bought 6d stamps instead, cut them in half, and was now asking Benn to authorise their passage through the postal service. Benn said he should have stuck the whole 6d stamp on them, and written to him for a refund. A while later, Benn found out that this man was in fact a stamp dealer, and rather than thirty bills to post he had cut up 300 stamps, and then presumably sent 600 letters to himself. The dealer claimed they were now worth £15 each. Benn concluded that he ought to be prosecuted. On an earlier occasion, in October 1965, Benn held his regular MP's surgery in Bristol. The usual stuff: a woman who had fallen in the street and was thinking about compensation; a man worried about how rising rail charges would affect his ladder business; and a stamp collector whose first-day cover had been ruined in the post.

I met Tony Benn in 2004, and he told me that his tenure as Postmaster-General had been one of his happiest times in government. He was proud of his achievements in liberating stamps from the rather fusty, official things they had been into the colourful and free-spirited items they became. I asked him about the Post Office Tower, which had gone up during his time as PMG. He told me about the opening, which had been attended not only by Harold Wilson but also by Sir Billy Butlin, who ran the revolving restaurant at the top. He told me about accompanying the Queen up to it a few weeks later. And then he mentioned the revolving restaurant again, and what a shame it was that it was no longer open to the public, and no longer still revolving. 'It was as much a part of sixties London as . . .' (my mind raced: a Labour government? The Grosvenor Square riots? The LSE protests?) '. . . the mini-skirt,' he said.

By the beginning of 1966 Tony Benn and the Stamp Advisory Committee had decided that Great Britain should have special stamps for Christmas 1966, and if these were a success, the issue would be repeated every year. I can't remember exactly what he said when he launched the *Blue Peter* competition, or whether he had been asked to leave his pipe in his pocket while addressing the young, but I can remember the excitement of the announcement. I – and of course Val and John and Tony were always addressing me directly – could make something that would be sent all over the world. There was probably an age limit, and I qualified. Millions of copies of my stamp would be printed, and my name would be on it (alone among PMGs, Tony Benn had insisted that the artists get full credit on their work). Simon Garfield. Perhaps even Simon Frank Garfield, or just S. F. Garfield, and in this way I would join the pantheon: David Gentleman, Faith Jacques, Michael and Sylvia Goaman and Clive Abbott, the designer of the Post Office Tower stamps, stretching eventually all the way back to Henry Corbould, William Wyon and the Penny Black. By the summer of 1966 *Blue Peter* had taught me many things: how to clean Big Ben, the story of Thor Heyerdahl and his raft *Kon-Tiki*, how an appeal to collect 60,000 second-hand paperbacks bought one inshore lifeboat, and how to make fruit cream crunch (cardiac pudding, featuring tinned mandarins, crushed digestives and a Giza-size pyramid of whipped cream topped off with silver confectioner's balls). The show had also informed me there was indeed an animal beginning with the letter X, the Xoloitzcuintli dog, currently trading as the Mexican Hairless. John and Valerie ran through the Christmas stamp rules. Entries did not have to be stamp-size, for they would be scaled down, but they did have to be 3.3 by 6 inches for an oblong stamp, 5.9 by 3.4 inches for an upright stamp. The designs had to illustrate either a festive or religious theme. There could be no lettering on the designs. Up to five colours could be used, but no dark colours please. Space should be left for the Queen's head and denomination, to be added at a later stage by the Post Office. And the entry had to be accompanied by a note from a head teacher saying that the design was the child's unaided work. Entries in by 20 June.

The rules were exacting but the possibilities limitless. After a great many programmes in which the presenters told the young viewer precisely what to do (which is why most parents favoured the show; it had nailed the concept of contained fun; adventure with discipline) I found the freedom to do whatever I wanted extremely daunting, almost stultifying. But one great idea was all I needed. I don't think I did many sketches or roughs of my stamp; I was perfectly content with my rule-busting brain-wave of sticking the Queen's profile on a traditional wintry image – a snowman's body – and leaving it at that. I think my mother thought it was an exceptional concept and helped me with the submission envelope and teacher's note, and from there it was just a case of waiting for the big news a few weeks later. But weeks passed, and still no news.

The judges were my heroes: Abbott, Gentleman, the Goamans and four others, but they took until October to decide. They chose a boy called James Berry, age six, from Beckenham in Kent, who had drawn a picture of an ordinary snowman with a red scarf and a pink hat. And a girl, also six, from Stafford in Staffordshire, who had painted the head of a king with rosy cheeks and a colourful crown. Her name was Tasveer Shemza, and she had won the greatest prize. Both Tasveer and James got £20 and a gold *Blue Peter* badge. But Tasveer's stamp had been selected as the key 3d issue, while James's design was on the 1s 6d. This meant that less than 11 million of James's stamp would be printed, but there would be 174 million of Tasveer's. It also meant that at the age of six Tasveer had become, from her family home in Stafford, Staffordshire, the bestselling British artist of all time. It was, quite simply, a miracle to me, and of course I felt madly jealous. But when Tasveer appeared on screen in a red and blue top similar to the colours on her stamp, I also felt that she was cute before that word was common, and I liked the way she held her brown toy koala bear for security. I had a bear just like that, almost certainly from the shop in London Zoo. Her stamp appeared on 1 December 1966, and it was vibrant, a king with jewels in his crown on a red background, with an embossed gold-foil profile of the Queen's head – victory for Tony Benn – which the unscrupulous soon discovered could be removed with chemicals or an iron. Within days of issue, many thousands were being circulated to dealers and at stamp fairs without the Queen's head, but as ironing would also remove the imprint of the embossing, the fakes were easy to spot. There were about 170 genuine missing-gold errors resulting from a printing glitch at Harrison & Sons factory in High Wycombe, but soon a far more available error emerged. At the foot of some stamps the initial 'T' for Tasveer had disappeared, leaving only her surname. This was probably caused by a speck of dirt covering the letter on the printing roller, and although it was not a spectacular error, it was an unusual one for a British stamp. It was also the first and only error that I actually received through the post.

It is difficult to convey just how exceptional this is – the equivalent for the error collector of finding a Renoir in a junk shop, although rather less valuable. To find that you had an error in your collection that you didn't have to buy above face value would only occur once in a collector's lifetime. Indeed, it has never occurred for me again. Unfortunately, it turned out (and very quickly) that there was one of these errors on almost every sheet of eighty stamps. Six rows down, two stamps in, and there it was, or rather wasn't: the infamous missing 'T'. One had a one-in-eighty chance of getting it, which, given the amount of mail sent using the 3d stamp, meant that the odds were very favourable. Many of these errors went unnoticed for eight weeks, and were thus thrown away or sent back to *Blue Peter* as part of its used stamp charity appeal, but then the February edition of *Gibbons Stamp Monthly* appeared. The column entitled 'Through the Magnifying Glass' reported 'shoals' of letters identifying the error, but the very first was reported by telephone – such was the urgency – by a certain K. Labbett, who just happened to be my kindergarten teacher.

The error went unnoticed by John Noakes. When Tasveer's victory was written up in the *Blue Peter* book of 1967, Noakes was pictured looking over the shoulder of a young checker called Jenny at the High Wycombe printing press. She had a large sheet of eighty stamps on the table in front of her, but it was also a high sheet, as beneath it there were fifty other sheets just the same. Behind her, in what looked like an airless and charmless room crammed with heavy metal furniture and very bored personnel, were three other women doing just the same. What were they thinking of as they checked more than two million sheets? According to Noakes, they were flicking through at the same speed as a bank cashier counts banknotes. 'But they weren't counting. They were checking.' They were checking, Noakes explained, because 'a fault in a stamp is what all collectors dream of. It could convert a 3d stamp into something worth thousands of pounds.' At one point during the *Blue Peter* visit, Jenny pulled a sheet to one side, the reject pile. It took Noakes about five minutes to spot what was wrong with it, and then he found it: a slight misalignment of perforations. Noakes told viewers that the faster Jenny flicked, the easier it was for her to find an error, something which seemed to make good sense at the time but now something I don't quite understand. At any rate, Jenny and all of her colleagues missed the missing 'T' flaw on every sheet they looked at, which gave the error collector enormous hope for the future.

Tasveer's stamp, which appeared in the Gibbons catalogue as SG 713 'King of the Orient', a name she had not given it herself, did not meet with universal approval. Many collectors couldn't understand how a stamp could possibly be designed by a child. In December 1966, the *Stamp Magazine* ran a letter describing them as 'gaudy monstrosities'. The following month

H. Elliot Pearse, of the World Association of Young Stamp Collectors, argued that, to the contrary, both Tasveer's and James's stamps showed the true spirit of seasonal goodwill. He believed the Postmaster-General was 'inspired', and although the stamps 'may appear crude when compared with our usual issues, they have opened up an entirely new field'. Two months later the debate raged on, and the tone had again become disapproving. This time, D. T. Phillips from Balcombe, Sussex, spoke for many of his colleagues in GB philatelic societies: 'The great majority of collectors – and indeed of the general public with whom I have discussed the matter – have either regarded these Christmas stamps, especially the 3d value, as a joke or as something far better suited to adorn a Christmas cracker than to represent Great Britain all over the world! Let us face it . . . they are only suitable for the nursery!' They didn't much like the runner-up designs either. When these appeared in the *Philatelic Bulletin* in December 1966, mine was not among them. Brenda Cooper's design featured a person at a piano and a choir of three. Lucy Richardson sent in three snowmen. Sarah L. Nash submitted a goose. Stephen Conroy sent in a snowman going downhill on a sled, smoking. And Tejinderjit Singh featured a snowman dressed as a clown.

That Christmas the Post Office received more than forty thousand letters addressed to Father Christmas at the North Pole. Rather than delivering them, they were put away somewhere, and possibly disposed of in a bin. Everyone who wrote got a reply from 'Reindeerland' in photocopied handscript with one of Tasveer Shemza's stamps in the corner:

My dear young friend,
Thank you for writing to me. My team of gnomes has been working very hard making all sorts of toys ready for Christmas. Of course

there may be something they have not thought of, but when I load my sledge I will do my best to see that you get the presents you would like.

I hope you have a very happy Christmas,
Santa

I met Tasveer Shemza forty years after I had seen her on television, and I would like to say she hadn't changed a bit. Certainly she was instantly recognisable by her hair, hazel brown in a Louise Brooks bob, then as now. Also, although she had recently turned forty-seven, she was still fairly small, and her cheeks still rosied up when she smiled. I liked her instantly, especially her slight nervousness and her willingness to please, and when I told her that I found her very attractive when I saw her on television in 1966 she said, 'Surely not.'

She sat in her office at Sussex Downs College, near Eastbourne. The only thing that wasn't so good was her memory. She couldn't, for instance, remember much about entering the competition, or the day she heard the news she had won. She wasn't sure whether she had any help with the design from her parents, which would have disqualified her, although the statute of limitations had long passed when she said, 'But if you look at it now, it does have a very nice border, hasn't it, the top blue bit and the red background – it is rather professional . . .'

She was an only child. Her parents were both art teachers. She already had all the inks and paints at home, and as well as the winning entry she thinks she may also have submitted a picture of an angel with odd wings and curly blonde hair.

'Any snowmen?'

'No, although the snow in 1964 was pretty impressive, wasn't it, so perhaps snow had made a big impression on a lot of kids. I don't know how I got the idea of doing a king's head, although it was basically my dad. I don't know if this was intentional or not, but it was very much what he looked like, very stylised facial hair, actually quite a typical Muslim beard [she runs her fingers over own chin as she describes it], nicely trimmed. And he always used to wear a hat in the morning to hold his hair down, and stop it flying all over, rather like the crown of course.'

I was taken by the idea, shrouded until now, that Great Britain's first Christmas stamp was modelled on a Muslim. Her father left Pakistan in 1956, and went to the Slade school of art. He married Tasveer's English mother in 1958, and Tasveer was born in Stafford a year later, where her parents both worked in local schools.

'I went to a girls' grammar school where it was expected that you went to university. I was an atheist, and I got the Religious Studies Prize.' She then went to York University, where she saved her grant in term-time to go travelling in the holidays. She trained to teach English as a foreign language, and now teaches others to become teachers. She met her husband in Egypt, and they now have two daughters who have long out-grown *Blue Peter*.

'It was all very nice indeed in the studio,' she says. 'Val Singleton I remember well, more than John Noakes. Just before we went on air, Val asked me how I got such shiny hair. And the producer – was it Libby Purves?'

'Perhaps Biddy Baxter?'

'Biddy Baxter – that's it. Libby, Biddy, similar. She was a lovely woman.'

The official prizegiving, another photocall, was held at the Post Office Tower. 'We went to the revolving restaurant and had fish and chips, and I was shocked and scandalised. There was me and James Berry, who was my age, and there was also a teenage girl who did the design of the first-day cover. I thought she may also have done a parcel stamp. She seemed terribly much older to us. She's almost been written out of the story. So we had fish and chips, and she licked the ketchup bottle. I was so shocked – I couldn't believe it. That's my strongest memory of the whole thing.'

For several years after her stamp was selected, Tasveer received a large amount of correspondence from collectors asking her for a signed photograph ('Good Wishes from Tasveer Shemza') or a signed first-day cover. In return, she would receive stamps from foreign countries or other gifts. When she got married she decided to keep her maiden name. 'I think it's a fantastic name – Tasveer Shemza, it goes together. And I was of that feminist generation where people thought, "Why would you change your name?" Also, my husband's name is Hodgson, he's a Yorkshireman, and I don't think that would go at all.

'Every so often people would come up to me and say, "You're the . . ." and they'd tell me what they could remember about the stamp. As I became a teenager I would become quite embarrassed about it. That normal teenage thing of being self-conscious. And it took me until I had kids of my own to not be embarrassed about it. Now I think it's a really fantastic achievement for a child.'

In 2005, one of my two sons almost appeared on a British Christmas stamp. Or at least he appeared in the *Royal Mail Yearbook* promoting the Christmas stamps, which is not quite as good, but distinctly closer than most people get.

In 1990, when my son Ben was two, the artist Catherine Yass took a photograph of him in my arms in a darkening street in South End Green, north London, where I lived. It was a chilly evening. I had a maroon jacket, and Ben was wearing a very large blue sweatshirt. Yass, a friend for about fifteen years, was the cousin of my first long-term girlfriend, and in the years I had known her she had experimented with many artforms, including sculpture and film. Her big breakthrough came with her photography, lightboxes and film, and in particular a signature technique in which she overlays a positive and a negative image of the same scene, heightening and deepening colours in the process. She had employed this to stunning effect in studies of graveyards, hospitals and portraits of Indian film stars, and in 2002 she was shortlisted for the Turner Prize. One of my favourite works was not a photograph but a looped video in which she sat facing the camera as she recited a long list of jokes in a mirthless and deadpan way. Two Jewish women meet in the street and one says gosh you look wonderful what have you been up to. The other replies I'm having an affair. Her friend says an affair how wonderful, who's doing the catering? A beggar stops a man in the street and says I haven't had any food for so long I've forgotten what it tastes like. The man says don't worry it still tastes the same.

Yass, who is in her early forties, first came to the attention of the Royal Mail in 1999. One day in late summer she received a call asking whether she'd be interested in designing a Christmas stamp. Christmas stamps are always special, but this year particularly so. They were the Christmas stamps of the Millennium Series, a sequence of ninety-six stamps released as four stamps each month for two years. It was the most ambitious stamp issue ever undertaken, and each one was commissioned from a leading artist. Yass was in good company: David Hockney, Bridget Riley, Howard Hodgkin, Patrick Caulfield, Ralph Steadman, Anthony Gormley, Craigie Aitchison, Don McCullin. They were chosen to illustrate a particular theme or achievement in Britain's past – The Farmers' Tale, The

Scientists' Tale, The Citizens' Tale, The Entertainers' Tale, The Travellers' Tale.

'For some reason,' Yass told me one day at her studio near Brick Lane in east London, 'I'm always asked to do Christmas projects. The stamp, the Christmas page in the *Royal Mail Yearbook*, decorating the Tate Christmas tree.' Yass is Jewish. I told her that it was Britain's modern institutional way of being multiculural without a big song and dance. I told her I was proud of my discovery that the first British Christmas stamp was based on a Muslim. Unlike Tasveer Shemza, Yass said she was disappointed that her stamp was to be used for overseas postage, rather than second or first class inland. But she was pleased that more people would become familiar with her art than ever before. 'Licking my work,' she said. 'You don't get more intimate than that.'

The stamp, which cost forty-four pence and marked the St Andrews pilgrimage, depicted the ruins of a church wall in gold and midnight blue. Yass showed me the many photographs and layers that went into its design, recalling how a person from Royal Mail had been particularly helpful in computer manipulation, and in turning the night-time into a thick velvety blue.

Six years later she was commissioned again. This time they didn't want a stamp, but an image they could use on a spread in the 2005 *Yearbook*, an annual gathering of all the year's stamps in one 'lavishly illustrated volume'. This was of interest predominantly to desperate completists and grandparents, but it wasn't thrown together as an afterthought; each of the year's stamps – in 2005 these included studies of Magic, *Jane Eyre* and Classic ITV – not only had a little biography about the designers, but also some illuminating essays about the theme. Catherine Yass's brief was to produce an image to accompany the theme of Madonna and Child. Because she is not a conventional artist, Yass suggested an original image: a father and child. Rather than take some new portraits, she retrieved an older image she had taken some years before: me and my son Ben in the dusk near a traffic island. The absence of a woman in this picture caused a frisson of tension at Royal Mail, fearful, perhaps, of the *Daily Mail*. A conflict was averted when Yass came up with a compromise: you wouldn't see the man. So my son is being held by someone, and you can see the holder's shoulder, but that's it. It's still a poignant moment for me, far more so than for my son, who isn't particularly interested in yearbooks. But there is my clothed shoulder on an image issued by the Royal Mail, a remote outpost in the long and distinguished journey of philately.

Shortly before I had visited Yass in her studio, I had heard other tales of millennium and Christmas stamps from Andrew Davidson, the illustrator best known (beyond the stamp world) for his illustrations for Ted Hughes's *The Iron Man*. Unlike Yass, who was an artist who derived most of her income from project grants and gallery shows, Davidson was a graphic illustrator by training and profession, a specialist in distilling essences from corporate mission statements. Designing stamps had become a habit he was keen to foster, for his reputation and sanity as well as his income.

I met Davidson at the British Postal Museum and Archive around the back of the Mount Pleasant sorting office near King's Cross, and he was instantly likeable. He was a Scotsman nearing his fifties, and he had a large balding pate and clear smile. He was a traditional craftsman, full of enthusiasms, a man who worked in a timber studio in his Cotswold garden, ideally with Radio 4 and a nice chunk of English boxwood to be engraved with spitstickers and scorpers. His woodcuts had graced envelopes and collections for fifteen years – Sherlock Holmes, ice-age animals, Robert the Bruce at the Battle of Bannockburn – and had led him to a theory about how to make a good postage stamp. You needed a good brief, an intellectual challenge. One benefited from well-researched references. One needed a large amount of inspiration, and respect for the subject matter. Experience helped, as did a knowledge of the principles of design, because 'it's not just a bit of perforated paper with the Queen's head in the corner and some picture placed in the space that's left'.

Like other solitary toilers, Davidson had mischievous streaks. There is something about traditional and painstaking design that invites subversion: the Huntley & Palmers biscuit tin with fornicating dogs in the bushes,* the top-secret film scripts that deliberately contain a different error in each one so that any leakages online can be easily traced to an individual. Davidson's triumph came with his Sherlock Holmes stamps of 1993. These were intricate designs, five stamps commemorating the centenary of the publication of 'The Final Problem', and they left plenty of room for creative manoeuvre. On the illustration for 'The Six Napoleons' stamp, depicting the scene where Holmes smashes a bust with a riding crop to find the black pearl, Davidson placed a piece of twisty pasta among the ceramic shards. On 'The Reigate Squire' he put something among the folds of the rug, 'but by this time the Royal Mail had found out what I was doing and asked me to get rid of the syringe.'

---

* A disgruntled illustrator, recently handed his notice of dismissal, added a few unusual touches to the design of a gay summer picnic scene that were not spotted until the tins appeared on the shelves (or so the story goes). Another highlight of this work was a jam-jar labelled 'shit'.

But it wasn't all fun. Davidson had crushing accounts of stamps commissioned but never issued, a Pond Life set, a Holiday Postcards set, a Brontë set, and he consoled himself as best he could: 'Because yours isn't adopted, it doesn't mean it's rubbish. It means that perhaps another set works better in the series through the year, or it may be politically sensitive. It's nothing personal.'

When he was growing up his one of his heroes was David Gentleman, who designed Churchill and the Battle of Britain in the mid-1960s. He says he'd be happy to be considered even in the same paragraph as Gentleman. Stamps bring him great joy, he says, and he delights in the happiness they bring to others. 'You know when you're on a long train journey and someone says, "What do you do, then?" I can reach for my wallet and take out some stamps and say, "This is what I do." I had a meeting a few weeks ago with a hugely important chap from Switzerland, and I showed him a set of these Ice Age stamps [the sabre-tooth cat, giant deer, woolly rhino, woolly mammoth and cave bear], and I laid them out on a table in front of him and he was thrilled. I said, "You can have them, they didn't cost me much."'

Andrew Davidson appeared to me to be a kind and generous man, and one who would not say a word against his employers in public. But at a lecture in the autumn of 2006 he stood up for his fellow designers and, with incredulity and dismay, showed a photo of an envelope carrying a label one can print from the Internet at home, just bar codes and other writing, no illustration, no creative thought or graphic design to speak of.

The country that invented stamps was now forging ahead with SmartStamp, something that swept away the need for the security printing presses of De La Rue in London, High Wycombe and Basingstoke, a domestic franking service that had stepped out of the office into every home with a computer. The adverts heralded a breakthrough: 'Print out the exact postage you need . . . mail-merge contacts from your PC's address book . . . manage how much you're spending on postage 24/7.'*

This seemed to me to be in direct conflict with the stated aims of the Royal Mail's Special Stamps programme, which, at the time of Catherine Yass and Andrew Davidson's work, was to: Commemorate important anniversaries; reflect the British contribution to world affairs, especially to the Commonwealth and Europe, in a variety of fields of activity, including the arts and sciences; display the many and varied aspects of the British way of life; extend public patronage to the arts by encouraging the development of minuscule art.

The biggest problem with SmartStamp, of course, is that it is not a stamp. With a printing press in every home, fewer people each year would buy or see artworks in minuscule, and the noble patronage of Tasveer Shemza, Yass and Davidson would slide away. A stamp no longer used for postage would become that dread thing: 'a collector's item', like those many useless things sold in newspaper magazines, an item produced solely for profit. Stamp collectors have seen this pattern emerging for many years, and SmartStamp made me feel that I wasn't a collector any more, but an owner and a sucker.

---

* The most surprising thing about the adverts for SmartStamp was the small print. This contained details of a special offer – try SmartStamp free for three months and if you don't love it you'll get your money back. Beneath this it stated: 'SmartStamp, Royal Mail, the Cruciform and the colour red are registered trade marks of Royal Mail Group plc.' It owned the colour red: no wonder its monopoly was taken away.

Mounts Long Dry

At the end of 2006, Royal Mail confirmed its stamp programme for 2007. There were to be eighteen new issues, an absolute nightmare for the completist. The Beatles. Sea Life. The Sky at Night. World of Invention. Wales. The Abolition of the Slave Trade. Celebrating England. Wembley Stadium. Beside the Seaside. Fortieth Anniversary of the Machin. Grand Prix. Scouts. Lest We Forget (Part 2). Endangered Species: Birds. British Army Uniform. The Queen's Sixtieth Wedding Anniversary. Christmas. And then a few months into the year, a new set was added to the list, the finest example yet of Royal Mail's matchless (although obvious) grasp on marketing: Harry Potter stamps, marking the publication in July 2007 of the final book. There were to be seven first-class stamps, each showing a different book jacket. There was also a miniature sheet containing five other stamps (the school crest of Hogwarts school and its four houses), as well as a Generic Smilers sheet, a collection of twenty stamps attached to labels featuring magic spells from the Harry Potter books, which are only revealed when warmed by the palm of a hand. The whole package, including two first-day covers, was available from the Post Office for £19.40.

How did it come to this? When did it get to the point where smitten and loyal collectors felt they were being fleeced? These issues were not a nightmare for collectors in the old-fashioned sense. There were no 'difficult' stamps among them, stamps that were hard to locate. The Royal Mail philatelic HQ at Tallents House in Edinburgh would have no problem sending them to you in several different formats (neat stamps, first-day cover, presentation pack, mini-sheets, 'prestige' booklet, complete sheets) and you'd be charged a handling fee for it. No, the nightmare was the cost. Some of the stamp values went as high as £1.19, most new issues would include six stamps, and in a year a collector could easily spend more than £100 trying to keep up with the basics. If you also wanted the new definitives and the multi-formats and special sheets and the yearbooks this would be several hundred pounds a year.

When I read about this forthcoming eighteen-set list I decided to end my direct debit with Royal Mail for an automatic purchase of every stamp. I had talked to friends who had done the same: my friend Paul Hersh had given up in 2000. The stamp magazines were full of letters from people saying things 'had got completely out of hand'.

The difficulty is, giving up collecting stamps is a very hard thing to do. When you stop looking forward, you stop believing in the future of stamps. I would like to be populist and optimistic about this, and I would like to think I am keeping things up to date for my grandchildren (as if they'd ever be remotely interested in stamps). And I like a lot of the new designs. I also had to acknowledge that giving up collecting stamps would not be a new thing for me, and it is usually regrettable. Fifty years ago, the postal historians L. N. and M. Williams noted that 'it has been held that unnecessary issues, that is to say, stamps that are not primarily issued for the pre-payment of postage, are choking philately and reducing its status . . .', but they also reasoned that new issues would encourage young people to enter the hobby. This argument is still advanced by Royal Mail today, not least when it issues such news-making sets as Harry Potter.

But who likes to be taken advantage of? Who likes to be told, in effect, 'you buy what we tell you to buy?' Is there any other hobby where obligation and habit compel you to buy things you don't like? With stamps it has ever been thus, and everyone has their breaking-point. On those rare occasions when I regret my decision I console myself with the knowledge that the stamps will never be rare, and my grandchildren could always buy them from a dealer at minimal mark-up. And then . . . and then I miss not owning the stamps.

The final straw for me came not with the list for 2007, but the possible list for 2009. In December 2006, collectors registered with Royal Mail received a voting card. The Stamp Committee had decided on 'nominations' for Special Stamps for 2009, and we could vote for the five we liked the sound of. We weren't voting for the designs, because they hadn't been designed yet. And there were no promises that anything suggested by collectors would make the final cut, but it was a goodwill attempt at democracy and public relations, and it was hard not to play along. There were thirty-six choices, including: The Theory of Evolution, Legendary Football Managers, Buses through The Ages, The National Association of Flower Arrangement Societies, Animal Heroes, Come Dancing and Horse Racing – The Sport of Kings. I could go on. Great British Opera. Universities of the UK. By Royal Appointment: Dress Designers. Crufts. The Universal Declaration of Human Rights. Comedians. And that wasn't the worst of it. The worst of it was the address to send your selections: The Data Solutions Centre, Manton Wood Enterprise Park, Worksop.

On the day I posted my choices, I made my first visit to the Royal Mail Archive around the back of the Mount Pleasant sorting office near King's Cross. The tagline on my admittance card said 'Our History through the Post', and they weren't mucking about. This was one thing Royal Mail did superbly well – protect and honour its past. It was home to the Reginald M. Phillips collection of Victorian stamps, one of the finest ever assembled. The main research room on the ground floor held the catalogues and journals, there was a little exhibition area with three glass cases showing how the Queen has been portrayed on stamps down the years, and then in the basement there were two storage areas. The first contained a few uniforms, some black-and-white photographs of postmen visiting lonely houses on remote hillsides, and many fantastic laminated posters (intricate designs for direct messages: 'Post Early for Christmas', 'Buy Your Radio Licence', 'Your Money Will Be Safe In Post Office Savings Bank – The Fritter Fly Will Get It If You Don't Look Out!'). But most of the space was occupied by vast shelves laden with document boxes relating to everything postal since the seventeenth century. Even the simplified catalogue ran to 212 pages, and made me feel very excited and very small. There were records about postmen and the owners of sub-post offices, and how much they received in pensions. There were thirty-seven volumes on Post Office property and income tax assessments between 1813 and 1891. There were 106 volumes on the conveyance of mail by railways, from three years before this service began in 1830, to 1975. I wanted to spend some time with the history of Post Office counters (106 volumes), and I could have passed a happy week with the private papers of Rowland Hill from 1836 to 1879. But there were other things to explore, not least the second basement room.

This room contained stamps, stamp designs, and stamp designs that were never issued. My tour guide talked about the ideal temperature control of 17.5 degrees Celsius and 50 per cent humidity, and said that the contents were so valuable that every time a staff member visited the stamp room there had to be another staff member present at all times. And then both of them would be continually filmed by the security cameras. It so happened that my guide had a phobia about lifts, and she had to run up or run down the stairs to be there whenever the lift opened with a new batch of visitors. I told her about Melanie Kilim and the Post Office Tower and I think it made her feel better.

A few weeks later, at the end of May 2006, I flew to Washington DC for the biggest stamp show in the world that year, and probably of all time. The World Philatelic Exhibition was held every ten years, and was billed in its advertisements as 'Stamps – and so much more!' Actually, it was almost all stamps. The big marketing plan was to encourage attendance from people who did not normally think of themselves as collectors, especially the young. There was to be a personal appearance from someone dressed as Postman Pat, and also from someone dressed as his American equivalent Mr Zip. Benjamin Franklin would also show up, and there would be special children's competitions and stamp camps, but in the main it would be men with grey hair and their gigantic wives.

It was a wonderful show. About 85,000 people turned up to buy from 160 dealers and see the 3,800 exhibition frames. Every obsession was catered for, and although the show lasted a week, no individual could possibly hope to study them all. Among the leading competitive displays from British exhibitors, all of which won either a gold medal or a 'large' gold medal from the international judges, there were entries on Norfolk postal history, the British occupation of Iraq, Zanzibar postal dues and a thematic show on bicycles.

The exhibits were open to all, but in another section of the Convention Center there was a vast amount of meeting behind closed doors. Clubs and societies had chosen the Washington show as an ideal place to hold their annual get-togethers, and the breadth of their coverage would have astonished the first Victorian collectors. Sitting down on just one day were the Haiti Philatelic Society, the Hong Kong Study Circle, the Society of Israel Philatelists, the Scandinavian Collectors Club, the International Society of Guatemala Collectors, the Canadian Society of Russian Philately, the Ottoman and Near East Philatelic Society, and the Scouts on Stamps Society.

The problem was, you attended these and you'd miss many other things, including workshops and presentations called 'What's in Your Attic?', 'Thinking about Thailand' by T. P. McDermott and 'Collecting Zeppelin Mail for the Price of Lunch' by Bob Horn. I was sorry to miss the talk by Dr Lubomir Floch and Miroslav Langhammer entitled '1993 Division of Czechoslovakia Post into Czech and Slovak Posts', but happy to be elsewhere for 'How to Design an Israeli Stamp with Surprise Guests'. I was fairly sure I knew who these surprise guests were going to be. They were going to be folk dancers. Every time Israel presents itself on an international stage there is an inevitable planeload of people in national costume dancing to 'Hava Nagila' or a song about the destruction of the Second Temple. In a small meeting room there will always be a lot of pressure to participate.

Later in the week it turned out that Bob Horn had a rival, a German man called Dietmar who was holding a talk on how to build a good Zeppelin collection, including 'crash and burn' mail from airships that were destroyed in combat. His talk began the awful way, with Dietmar asking everyone in the room to introduce themselves. 'I'm Bob Stranks from Albuquerque, I'm Jim Banks from New Falls . . .' Most of them seemed to know each other from specialist Zeppelin and crash mail seminars in the past. 'I'm Simon Garfield from London.' A couple glanced round with a look that said 'interloper'. I could definitely hear people whispering, 'Did he say Simon Garfunkel?'

'The main thing', Dietmar said, 'is research. But good research. It's no point doing what somebody else has just done. I mean you could do Switzerland, which is a lot of fun for you, but there's a catalogue zis zick [he held his thumb and forefinger about four inches apart]. So do something original – maybe about rates, or how the letter got to the airship, or perhaps collect letters from the staff on board, and when you have done your research please share it.' He also said that you can collect for twenty years, but it's only when you spend six months writing it up for an exhibition that you really begin to understand what you have.

The best crash and burn mail can reach colossal prices, and there were several expensive items on offer in the show's many auctions. They appeared in catalogues next to rarities from every nation, and the auctions were the first I had attended where the live action was occasionally interrupted by a 'ding' from the loudspeaker at the side of the auctioneer – the sign that someone had upped the bid on the Internet. No longer did one have to sweat it out in the room or on the phone; now one could buy a Cape of Good Hope fourpence woodblock, vermilion, error of colour, large margins, central faults and creased though not visible on the face – a rare opportunity to own a great rarity for £40,000 – just by sitting in an office or by a pool or Brent Cross car park and clicking Submit.

But the very rarest items were not for sale at any price with any technology. The Court of Honour, guarded by two members of the Washington police force, contained items collectively valued at millions of dollars, and few of them were pretty. But they were each unique, and they told stories that have passed into folklore.

My favourite was the Alexandria 'Blue Boy', a fifty-cent provisional stamp from 1847, the year that official government stamps were first issued in the United States. The stamp was issued on blue paper, and carries a circle of forty rosettes around the lettering 'Alexandria Post Office – Paid'. It is the only known example, loaned by a Swiss collector who agreed to let Washington have it for a week so long as Washington insured it for $5 million. But its appearance at this show was doubly unique. The stamp was attached to an envelope, and, for the first time after years of detective work, the innards of the envelope were also on display. This happened to be a love letter, of the most gentle sort, sent from a man called James Wallace Hooff to Jannett Hooff Brown. It was a forbidden love. They were twenty-four and twenty-three, and they were second cousins. They were also of different denominations, Presbyterian and Episcopalian. They lived in the same street in Richmond, Virginia, and the letter that was sent by James Hooff from Alexandria at the end of 1847 contained news of family events. By contemporary standards there isn't much in his writing to set the heart aflame, but there is a soft longing beneath the lines 'whenever you think you can write me a line without exciting the attention of your coz. Wash, do so, for it gives me a great deal of pleasure to receive a letter from you, even if it is only a short one'. He closes with a reminder of their fragile position: 'Bye the bye, I believe Aunt Julia has an idea of my writing you; for two or three days after my first letter to you, she wrote Mother. And Mother laughingly remarked "That if there was any love going on Aunt Julia was sure to find it out," and while making that remark, I think, looked at me, but I continued reading, as if what she said did not apply to me in the least.' (Six years later, with Aunt Julia no longer on the scene, they married and had three children.) Hooff signs off, 'Yours with the greatest affection, W', and below this lay an instruction: 'Burn as Usual.'

The other great American gem, valued at $3 million, was the 1868 one-cent Z Grill. This was once the property of Bill Gross, the man who we earlier saw auctioning off his Penny Blacks for Médecins sans Frontières. Gross is a sort of philatelic Barnum, pleased with what stamps can bring to the world of entertainment. In November 2005, Gross bought the unique plate-number block of the inverted twenty-four-cent Jenny airmail issue from 1918, the famous upside-down biplane error. He paid almost $3 million, but the purchase was only the means to an end. What he really wanted was the Z Grill – a blue, used line-engraved stamp showing Benjamin Franklin, valuable because it had a particular waffle-like security impression on the back to aid the absorption of cancellation ink.

Only two are known. The first is in the New York Public Library, and the second was bought at auction in 1998 for $935,000 (the purchaser, Don Sundman of the Mystic Stamp Company, encouraged his eleven-year-old son to raise his bidding paddle). Bill Gross owned every nineteenth-century American stamp apart from the Z Grill, and organised the swap of his Jenny error block to complete his collection. And so here it was in Washington, heavily guarded, sealed beneath perspex and glass, the most expensive single stamp in the world.

With all this on display, you needed a proper opening ceremony, and the Americans tend not to let you down on this sort of thing. The official start of the show included a procession of dignitaries from all over the world. In a written message, President George W. Bush sent his very best. We stood for a parade of flags, led by two little drummer boys from a company called Children of the American Revolution. We witnessed the dedication to the new Wonders of America stamps. We saw Doug Foote, a professional fancy dancer, jig his way across the stage to the beat of native drums and the White Oak Singers. Towards the end there was a young boy with Crohn's disease whose wish it was to meet the Postmaster General.

Sitting behind me at this ceremony was a plump, balding, genial-looking man with large glasses called Michael Sefi. He appeared both interested and bemused by the palaver, and probably rather pleased that they did things differently where he came from. He came from St James's Palace, the place where he holds what may be the best job in world philately – looking after the stamps of Queen Elizabeth II.

As Keeper of the Royal Philatelic Collection, Michael Sefi has responsibility for many hundreds of albums of GB and Commonwealth material. Effectively he looks after the stamps belonging to the woman who appears on all of them since 1953. There are so many stamps that they have never been counted, but they have been divided for ease of reference: the 328 red albums are the most valuable, containing material predominantly amassed by King George V. The blue collection contains material from the reign of King George VI, and the green collection covers the current reign. Collectively the albums make what is the most comprehensive collection of British and Commonwealth material in the world, and the most valuable. Most of the valuable objects in the royal palaces are held by the Queen in trust for her successors and the nation, unlike the Royal Philatelic Collection, which is owned by her privately. It is with her personal permission that it may be viewed by researchers and mounted in travelling exhibitions. One such exhibition had accompanied Michael Sefi across the ocean to Washington, and it contained several items to make you fall to your knees. There was an example of the 'Rainbow' proofs sent to Rowland Hill by the printers Perkins, Bacon and Petch suggesting possible alternative colours to the Penny Black, including the red shade that was finally selected. There were fascinating proofs and errors from the Falklands, Cayman Islands, Jamaica and British Guiana. But the most mouth-watering item was also one of the Royal Collection's latest acquisitions, the 'Kirkcudbright' cover from 6 May 1840, a wrapper bearing a block of ten lightly cancelled Penny Blacks sent on the first day of issue. There are about seventy known first-day covers from this date, but this is the only one with more than two stamps, addressed simply to James Burnie Esq., Kirkcudbright (pronounced kir-cu-bree). It is worth, at a conservative estimate, about £500,000.

Sefi spent the first days of the exhibition milling around the Court of Honour and the National Postal Museum stands talking to old friends and answering questions from the public. He explained that the Kirkcudbright cover was bought in 2001, but only after discussions with the Privy Purse concluded that it would be necessary to offset the cost by selling some duplicates. He also talked about the dangers of light, and the ideal 'five-foot candle standard' (or fifty lux) that protects fugitive inks from fading or becoming unstable. This might be a little dim for those familiar only with less valuable displays, but it is a key factor in ensuring the protection of the rarest material.

The low light also generates a certain hushed reverence around the stamps, something their owners and trustees are keen to encourage.

A while later I called on Michael Sefi in his office in St James's Palace. He had emailed me a hand-drawn map to help me find it, and an accompanying note stating, in capitals, 'Do not go to Buckingham Palace – we are not there!'

The office resembled a collector's study, the walls heavy with auction catalogues and reference books. There was also somebody called Colette Saunders in the room, from the Buckingham Palace press office, presumably installed to ensure I didn't ask anything unseemly about the Queen and to limit the chances of Sefi revealing any terrible secrets. In fact, he had met the Queen only fleetingly; her interest in philately was not quite what her grandfather's had been.

I had come to talk about the responsibility of managing the most impressive private stamp collection in the world, but I also wanted to ask about a collector's motivation, and in so doing learn more about myself.

Sefi is not only a curator and a philatelic scholar, but a collector too, and the arc of his passion seemed to reflect my own. He was born in London, and began collecting as a schoolboy in the late 1940s. He was particularly interested in the pictures on colonial stamps, and he remembers a lot of landscapes and animals from exotic places he had no expectation of ever visiting. 'Tanganyika, Kenya, Uganda,' he says. 'And Fiji, for example. Who on earth went to Fiji? To a ten year old I don't think jingoism is a word that means very much, but even in the late forties large parts of the world were red on the map. And so you saw stamps with the monarch on, George VI and then the Queen, and this somehow connected back to the home country.' His father wasn't a collector, but his grandfather was, and although he sold his main collection just after the war, there was a second or third collection which he gave to his grandson, mostly poor and used copies of Great Britain and Commonwealth. 'But they delighted my eye.'

Sefi wonders whether this is why young people are less interested in stamp collecting today – in an age of email and cheap air travel, their origins hold no mystery. But there are other reasons. 'Undoubtedly there is a lost generation in collecting. I initially went to a day school, and there were after-school clubs often led by teachers, and many boys joined the stamp club. But then there was a period where the teaching profession effectively withdrew from that sort of thing. So there is a whole generation where young people were never exposed to stamps, and we are now into a second or third generation where the teachers themselves have not been exposed.'

His interest waned from the age of thirteen – examinations and then girls. And then: I knew almost exactly what he was going to say, because it was the template I once thought I had sketched uniquely for myself. You come back. Like a spark in a garage that sets the house alight, something ignites to send you spiralling back to a love you thought you had quelled. You think: there must be something more to life than this (whatever it is: kids, job, materialism). As an alternative to religion and spirituality there are stamps, the quiet ordering of a life, the old-fashioned way of shutting out the world while bestowing it with meaning.

'Simple story really,' Sefi says. 'One of my children's godparents gave the child a Stanley Gibbons starter album. The child was nine, I suppose. I saw this and said, "Oh yes, stamps, I've got some in the loft." Instant turn-off as far as the child was concerned, but I pulled down the suitcase, which I had hardly looked at since I was thirteen, and noticed that some of the special valuable items that I had put to one side had disappeared. Penny Blacks. Twopenny Blues. Some Danish stamps. Don't know what happened to them. I had kept them in a special little stockbook, and that had vanished. Vanished. I get quite upset when I look at prices they reach today – the Danish five-kroner stamp of 1912 unused is today catalogued at £200. So I started re-looking at some of it, particularly the Great Britain George V period, and it took off from there.'

This was at the end of the seventies, with Sefi in his late thirties. He was a partner in a firm of chartered accountants which merged with the company that is now Deloitte. He was a taxation specialist and faced a demanding schedule, often working on weekends. He found stamps to be a relaxing diversion, but also one where he used his brain. 'I think my wife felt it was a good way of keeping me out of mischief, and it meant I wasn't spending money on wine, women and song. But little do wives know how much men spend on their hobbies.'

He soon found an interesting and manageable specialisation – the GB 'Downey Head' stamps issued in June 1911 to co-incide with George V's coronation. The stamps were not well received, particularly the three-quarter profile of the monarch from the Court photographers W. & D. Downey replacing the standard side-on view. The stamps – a green halfpenny and a red penny – were replaced after less than two years, but in that time a large amount of plate, watermark and shade variations arose to make a study of the stamp rewarding. The period of sale also marked the climax of the universal penny post, with envelopes still going all over the world for the same cost as in 1840. Collecting these stamps and covers was also not too expensive. 'If you want a bottom row of a common Downey

Head printing you'd pay £60 or £70,' Sefi says. 'In contrast to what you'd have to pay for a complete King Edward VII bottom row, no contest. But of course coming here to some extent takes the shine off my collection. I do have one or two things the King didn't have, for instance I've got some bigger pieces of the 1912 paper trials, but yes, coming here was a bit of a . . . and no, I haven't done swaps, and nor would I.'

The King he refers to is George V, the Collector King, a man who would spend three afternoons a week on his collection when he was in London, and whose interest in stamps began long before he began appearing on them.

He was not the first to contribute to the Royal Collection – the first important item in the albums dates from 1856, when the Prince of Wales and his younger brother Albert visited the De La Rue printing firm and came home with panes of the newest 6d stamps. Albert later became serious about stamp collecting, serving as Honorary President of the leading London Philatelic Society, but George V was the first to become consumed by it. His dedication has provided succour to all besieged or self-doubting collectors who followed him: stamp collecting was the Hobby of Kings; if it was good enough for the monarch, who would dare say it was a trivial or wasteful pastime?

He began collecting before he ascended the throne, first as Prince George of Wales and then as Duke of York. He probably couldn't believe the stars when he succeeded his father as king on 6 May 1910, precisely the seventieth anniversary of the Penny Black. His letters and journals describe an advanced desire: on an official trip to Australia and New Zealand as the Duke of York in 1901, it is clear that much pleasure from the journey derived from acquiring new stamps from dealers and local societies. Several afternoons on board HMS *Ophir* are spent laying out and protecting new additions. His reputation as a collector was already well established wherever he travelled. In Sydney, the local philatelic club presented him with a leather-bound volume with many current and classic stamps; the genuine tone of the thank-you letter written by his equerry, himself a philatelist, suggested that he was more delighted with the gift than a hundred engraved bowls he had gathered elsewhere. In February 1908, two years before becoming king, George wrote to a friend regarding the purchase of some stamps from Barbados. The letter outlined his ultimate purpose. 'But remember, I wish to have the *best* collection & not *one* of the best collections in England, therefore if you think that there are a few more stamps required to make it so don't hesitate to take them . . .' There was one stamp in particular he considered a key addition to the best collection in Britain: the Two Pence Post Office Blue Mauritius. His chance came in 1904, when an unused example came up for auction at the London auction house of Puttick and Simpson. What stood in the way of a future king and the stamp he coveted? Surely not money. Before the auction, George suggested to his philatelic adviser John Tilleard that he make an offer to the stamp's owner to withdraw it from auction for £1,200. The vendor declined, believing it would fetch more with multiple bidders. George wrote to Tilleard: 'I am still very anxious to have the stamp and now authorise you or an agent to bid for it at the auction up to £1,550 inclusive [of fees].' And then, a hint of self-doubt: 'I am particularly keen to buy the stamp although it does seem to be a great deal of money to give for it. I suppose of course you have seen the stamp & can guarantee that it is genuine.'

And so it was that a stamp issued in 1847 in time for Lady Gomm's ball, and regarded initially as an amusing and purely functionary aid to communication, was now the subject of fierce desire. A few days before the auction, barely able to contain his agitation, George wrote to his adviser once more. 'You can send me a telegram here [York Cottage] on Wednesday if you have secured the "Post Office". Better say merely "Stamp is yours" & write later full particulars.' He got it. Bidding anonymously against strong competition from German dealers, Tilleard's appointed agent was successful at £1,450, at the time the highest price ever paid for a single stamp. A short while later, reading of the price in a newspaper, one of George's staff asked whether he had seen that some 'damned fool' had paid that much for a single stamp. In fact, George was proud of his acquisition and the price he paid for it, and he often repeated this story at dinner parties. He later wrote to Tilleard: 'I am also very glad that I have kept it in England & prevented it going to Germany.' He asked Tilleard to keep it in his safe until he could call for it in London. 'I quite agree that you ought at once to increase the fire insurance on the collection.'

Michael Sefi is only the sixth keeper of the Royal Philatelic Collection in over ninety years. His path to the job began not long after he started collecting as an adult. He swiftly established himself as part of London's philatelic community, becoming treasurer and then president of the Great Britain Philatelic Society and spending fifteen years on the council of the Royal Philatelic Society. In 1996 he was asked by Charles Goodwyn, his predecessor at St James's Palace, to become his deputy, and he joined at a critical time. The monarchy had not been going through a good patch, and it was felt that the collection should be given greater exposure as part of an attempt to make the royal family more accessible. 'One has to be absolutely clear,' Sefi told me. 'The Royal Philatelic Collection is a private collection, the property of the Queen, although it is said she regards it as an heirloom. Periodically one is going to be challenged on the whole *raison d'être* of the collection and maintaining it.

'It would be quite simple for it to be said, "This is absurd. What on earth are we doing, for a relatively minority interest, spending the Queen's personal money on buying things? What we ought to be doing is closing the door. When anything new comes in we should just put it into the filing. Let's not worry about exhibitions, and why should we be bothered about a succession of researchers wanting to come to look at something particular?"'

'So every so often we must stop to think about what is the reason for this collection. Of course it has manifold purposes, quite apart from the publicity thing. Here is something that the monarchy is providing which is completely unrelated to government and the representational role of the monarchy, and which is doing good for the country. And then there is the researcher element. There is no question at all that there is a body of people out there who are studying particular areas, and we have material here which they can't access anywhere else.'

Sefi's time with the collection is spent writing up album pages, organising exhibitions and giving speeches about his work to societies. He does occasionally study the auction catalogues to see if there's anything that will improve what is already there, 'but you have to realise that certainly as far as pre-1936 is concerned, there are very few gaps indeed, and the kind of things that are missing never come on the market anyway'. The last time he purchased something significant was in 2005, a Cape of Good Hope item which cost £80,000. 'The problem is,' he says, 'with more modern material it is effectively open-ended. One could spend all day going through catalogues looking at GB error material and paying enormous prices for it.'

'And some of us do,' I told him. He regarded me with empathetic pity. I asked him about the Queen, and whether she shows any interest in the collection, in the many albums . . .

'I think it would be giving a false impression if one said she did. The Queen undoubtedly is very conscious that here is something for which she has a responsibility, and therefore does take an interest in what we do with it. She approves requests for items from the collection to go to exhibitions, and any significant purchases or sales.' And she approves every issue that bears her head or her cipher.

I asked him about the sale of royal stamps to finance the Kirkcudbright cover, and it turned into a little argument. 'We had to be quite careful,' he said. 'There were some items we were considering selling that it was felt the quality was such that reputationally they wouldn't do us any good and shouldn't be included in the sale. That arises because George V virtually never disposed of anything. I have the complete financial records here from about 1914 to his death, and virtually nothing was sold during that time. He was buying individual items and collections, he was improving things, but he wasn't disposing of what you and I would call spacefillers. So you can look at an album and see some real rubbish on the same page as some absolutely marvellous material. New Zealand springs to mind. I think actually that makes the collection poorer in some ways.'

'But it also makes it more interesting and more human,' I suggested. 'What you're seeing is the gestation of a collection.'

'Well, hmmm, yeessss. No. I don't think I agree. The Red Collection as we call it, the collection to 1936, which has between 15,000 to 18,000 pages, and they are all written up in the same hand, that of Sir Edward Bacon, I don't think having rubbish on the same page as quality, I don't think that makes the collection more human. Most serious collectors do trade on. I certainly have done that.'

'But it shows the King to be a hoarder, and a collector with faults, which is interesting in itself.'

'Personally perhaps. I doubt if this benefits the collection.'

I then asked him about where stamp collecting will be heading in the future.

'I think a more interesting question is, "What will people be doing with their leisure time?" It isn't just stamp collecting . . . Many leisure activities which have any sort of organisation attached to them find it increasingly difficult to get people who are prepared to take on board the responsibility of management that collecting demands – be that matchboxes or fans or stamps. The organisation can be a burden, people are much less regimented, and wish to be so, in their lives than they were in the fifties or sixties.' There were many reasons, he says, and the discipline encountered during the two great wars had much to do with it. 'One has memories of these vast fields full of people engaged in what I call physical jerks but I know has a grander name – calisthenics? All about regimentation. But now for good or bad today's population is thoroughly different in terms of approach. That leads to a very much more individualistic attitude. So those things that require organisations – and after all, stamp collecting is if nothing else a form of regimentation – is less attractive to people.'

Does that mean that in years to come the entire hobby will shrink to the size of a walnut?

'I don't know. In this country to some extent possibly, but abroad no. It's still very strong in some countries, especially in the Far East. You only had to be in Beijing in 1999 . . . All right, stamp collecting is a government-approved activity, but nevertheless there was a ten-day exhibition and the gates were closed every day because of the crowds, and there were some very angry Western exhibitors who were not able to get in. The queues for first-day covers from the Chinese Post Office were endless.

At the end of our conversation, I asked Michael Sefi the same thing I had asked when we met. Why do we collect? What is the instinct that propels us to a chosen life of trying to complete something we never can? 'I guess it has something to do with being a hunter-gatherer, the squirrel instinct as I prefer to call it,' Sefi said. 'My wife has said it's all about anal retention and potty training.' So it's mostly a male thing.

'No, I don't agree with that. I think women tend to collect more decorative things. An obvious example is fans . . . You could get very sexist and say that women are mostly interested in gathering things for the house. In stamp collecting there are a number of women who are very active in thematic collecting – cats or flowers or royalty.' Sefi thought there may be a genetic element to the debate, something that steers women in a different direction from men. He told me he had three grown-up children, two daughters and a younger son, and when they were smaller the son had all the options of hand-me-down dolls and girl playthings, but he immediately started collecting cars and Action Men. 'I was away working a lot when he was two or three, so I don't think it could be put down to parental conditioning.' Almost inevitably, his son, who is called Charles, is not such a keen collector as his father.

As I left and walked across the royal courtyard, a sadness fell upon me, as if I had just witnessed – or was indeed part of – the closing of an era. I felt as though I was in a dusk-descending poem by John Betjeman. And when I got home I remembered what the poem was – 'Death of King George V'. This described the demise of the great stamp king and the accession of Edward VIII, who was not a collector, and who had only four low-value British stamps issued in his name before he abdicated. Edward had no need for stamps: he had found the woman of his dreams.

Not for Sale

By far the most joyful working afternoon I have ever spent occurred in the summer of 1992. Very painfully, it was also the afternoon I made an irreversible error of judgement that I regret almost every time I visit an art gallery. Collectors delight in their acquisitions, but it is nothing compared to the agonies unleashed when something gets away. Rationally, one shouldn't care. But desire burns away, and gets deeper with time.

I had gone to Cork Street behind the Royal Academy to interview the art dealer John Kasmin about his final show. This was a significant moment – a clear announcement, as if anyone really needed telling, that modern art was in trouble. The recession that had first hit the property world had swiftly moved to the collecting world, stamps as well as art. For Kasmin to be selling up was indeed a milestone: a fixture of the art trade for almost forty years, Kasmin's decision to sell by appointment from home marked the end of . . . actually it just marked the end of Kasmin in Cork Street, but this was journalism and so there was a story to be made.

It was greed that ruined the art world, Kasmin told me not long after I had positioned my tape-recorder on a desk in the middle of the gallery. Kasmin was skittering about on parquet, putting prices up on the works for his show. He was a small man with big round glasses and an open-necked striped shirt, not quite sixty. He used a Bic Biro, and I made a mental note: times tough indeed!

'God, I should never have had a last show,' he said. 'Too many people get sentimental. I really should have done it several years ago. As the prices went up I found it an increasingly meaningless and silly activity. But partly you carry on by impetus, and you get spoilt when the money keeps coming in and it's easy to make.'

But then, in the dealer's phrase, 'the business just stopped. You've got to be very convinced of what you're doing in the face of no possibility of making money, only of losing.'

Value in art was like value in stamps. You couldn't eat off art, unless it was Julian Schnabel's smashed plates. When the bottom fell out of the art market, the market in stamps declined at the same time and for the same reasons – over-speculation and recession. Neither had intrinsic value beyond the price of postage and canvas. For too many people, an enjoyment of art and stamps declines proportionately alongside their value.

Kasmin told me that he always believed the cost of art had to have some sort of benchmark; his final show contained a large Stephen Buckley work in mixed media, and traditionally Kasmin had always priced Buckley's work in line with the cost of a new Mini, but now Minis were costing more and Buckley wasn't selling so fast. I asked him when things ceased to be fun for him. Kasmin called it 'Saatchi time . . . All these people in the eighties buying things to leave in warehouses. I began to feel less and less part of it because the money thing just wasn't my game. I don't like to be short of money, but I could never get *into* it. I always liked dealing with people who used it. You know, that old-fashioned thing: people putting art on the walls and looking at it.'

The good news was, there were now bargains to be had. Not

the sort of bargains that Kasmin once enjoyed – five Bacons for six grand. But very good value for the art lover so long as the art lover held their nerve. In Kasmin's last show there was a big John Hoyland painting – a painting, not a print, seems mad now – for £5,000. And there was a Hockney – which was a print, one of an edition of five early lithographs – going for £6,000. It was called *Fish and Chip Shop* and Hockney had made it in 1954, at the age of seventeen, when he was at Bradford Art School. The print showed the interior of a local chippy, a plump man in a white coat frying, a woman in an apron serving. She was serving a young blond man who looked rather like Hockney, except Hockney hadn't yet bleached his dark hair. It was a vivid, warm scene, with a skilful display of perspective. It was romantic, and I wanted it.

And £6,000 didn't seem like a lot for an early Hockney.* I could have put it on my MasterCard, and even if I didn't pay it off for years it would still have been a steal. But it seemed like a lot of money at the time, and far more than I had ever spent on anything apart from a house and car. Also, something honourable inside me told me that it would have been a little odd for a journalist to have bought it before the private view later that evening, which was obviously complete rubbish. So I didn't put it on my MasterCard. And when I came back the next day it had a red sticker next to it.

Kasmin's real name was John Kaye. He was born in Whitechapel, east London, in 1934. He grew up in Oxford, and at

---

* Kasmin told me: 'I don't expect anyone just to walk in off the street and buy it. And it's very difficult to know how to price it: £6,000 is a rounded figure because for a long time it's been the equivalent of $10,000. The proprietors [in the picture] were friends of Hockney's family. It's just a schoolboy work; you can't say it's a great work. It's mostly enjoyable in the light of what he later became.'

seventeen he fled to New Zealand to write poetry and escape his father. He became a sort of Kiwi beat, and made himself undesirable by trying to rob a bank. On his return to England he fell into art dealing via bohemian Soho, and soon established himself as someone with original taste; when Pop was all the rage, Kasmin said it was junk.

Kasmin was not gay: he was keen to tell me of his many, many successes with women in the mid-1950s when he was just starting out with the dealer Victor Musgrave. 'Nothing else to do but screw in those days. Certainly so little business.' But the man who walked in about twenty minutes after me was gay, something that was first visible to the general public from his earliest art in the 1950s.

'Here is Mr Hockney,' Kasmin announced as Hockney walked in from the street. He had come to say that he was too tired to attend the opening that evening, but he wanted to wish him good luck. He looked just like Hockney should: green shirt, red tie, beige baggy suit, two-tone suede and leather shoes, light blue raincoat, lime green umbrella, tortoiseshell glasses, and a hearing aid that was half bright blue and half bright red. He poured himself a mineral water in Kasmin's office. He was in from Los Angeles to see his mother and receive an honorary doctorate from the Royal College of Art.

Hockney (pulling up a chair): Being a doctor is not that much use really. You still can't write prescriptions for your own drugs. Someone asked me how it felt. I said, 'Take two aspirins and call me in the morning.'

Kasmin: I've hung up *Fish and Chip Shop*. Did you see it as you walked in? I thought, in a rather kinky show, why not have a kinky Hockney?

I'll miss having a place where people can drop by and see

what I've got. If I get really itchy and absolutely hate it I'll maybe open up a shop or a café. For now I think I'll just put my head down for a bit and become a collector. If you become a collector you get invited to all the parties. People say, will I still go abroad, and I say I won't need to any more. I used to go abroad only to run away from the gallery. I used to travel a lot with people like Bruce Chatwin. I used to love adventures. But now a lot of friends are dead. I'm going to another funeral of a great friend tomorrow, the architect who's always done my galleries. It takes the taste off things a wee bit.

Hockney (*patting Kasmin's stomach*): You're exercising, are you?

Kasmin: I've just been fed up by an old friend.

Hockney: You should exercise.

Kasmin: Since I've given up smoking and drinking I've taken up ice-cream.

Hockney (*horrified*): You'd be better off smoking than having ice-cream.

Kasmin: I like the ice-cream, thank you.

Hockney (*still outraged*): It's very bad for you.

Kasmin: I only eat it every now and then.

Hockney: It's solid fat!

   He pours himself more water and asks:
   Why am I drinking so much of this stuff?

Kasmin (*who once drank heavily*): My unaccustomed bout of sobriety has made me look at things in a completely new light and realise that I've been thrashing about a bit, going on showing what I always did, picking out good art, but no pacemakers. This is not a position to feed you, to make you want to go on into the headwind.

Hockney: I think it's all rather good now. It's like the art world is going back to being sane again.

Kasmin: The picture of yours that brought the most money at auction [*in May 1989*] you painted at art school. You painted it very, very big in order to get a bit of privacy. It was as big as a wall.

Hockney: I got paid £85 for it.

Kasmin: That was from me! I couldn't work out where to put it. It just fitted in the hallway of my little house off Fulham Road when I was dealing from home. I thought, what am I going to do with it? I finally sold it for £150 to a man who swore to me that it was going to his children's primary school. [*The picture was later sold on.*] Then at auction twenty-five years later it sold for $2.2 million to some mad lady in America.

Hockney (*wistfully*): It was called *A Grand Procession of Dignitaries*.

Kasmin: When are you coming back here again?

Hockney: Tomorrow, if you like.

Kasmin: No, coming *back*. To Britain.

Hockney: I'll be coming back to start the opera around 20 October. *Die Frau ohne Schatten* will hit the fans at Covent Garden on 16 November. Hit the fans. Get it? The *Schatten* will hit the fans.

Kasmin: Oh, the *Schatten*.

Hockney: That was a joke. I won't explain any more. Kas has no ear for music whatsoever.

This one afternoon in the presence of Kasmin and Hockney formed an obsession that later took on the form of a life's quest. Their conversation also assures me that I am not the only one to muse on inflation and opportunities lost.

Of course, it's not just about money. I'm not sure one ever forgives oneself for the errors one makes as a collector, and on that afternoon I made the greatest error possible, the classic mistake: I didn't buy something I loved. A few months later, the former *Time Out* art critic Sarah Kent told me that she had once done the same, and she was a professional. She also said that she might regret the non-purchase until she died.

I asked Kasmin if there was much of Hockney's work that he didn't like.

Kasmin: Of course. I go through periods when I don't like some of the stuff at all. But I don't actually hate it. Sometimes David doesn't like it, but he only doesn't like it afterwards. David changes so much. It would be impossible for one person to like everything he does.

Hockney: The only person who likes all kinds of art is an auctioneer.

Kasmin: Or your mother.

Hockney: Oh yes, my mother.

    They wander out of Kasmin's office. Hockney settles by 'Fish and Chip Shop'.

Kasmin: I always wondered, was that boy meant to be you, David? An idealised you?

Hockney: Kind of. Yes, I'm always leaning like that. It was always the husband who did the frying and the woman who did the serving. When I was younger I used to go into fish and chip shops late at night and say: 'Got any chips left?', and when they said yes, I'd say, 'Well, it's your own fault for cooking too many.'

Kasmin (*examining print*): You don't get vinegar shakers like that any more.

Hockney: You do in Bridlington.

Kasmin: The whole thing has a Vuillard feel to it.

Hockney: Any student doing a print like that in those days made it look like Vuillard.

Kasmin: Have you got a copy of it?

Hockney: I think so. Had to buy it, though.

With this horse's-mouth provenance, how on earth did I miss my chance? I asked myself this for nine years, from the moment I followed Hockney out of the gallery until the print – i.e. one of the five of them – came up for auction at Sotheby's in November 2001, and I was there with my paddle waiting for it. The collectors Reba and Dave Williams were selling their prints, Lucian Freud, Ben Nicholson and all. I was now more keen than ever on the lithograph that I had been introduced to by Kasmin and Hockney, and its greatness as a piece of art had probably grown in my mind beyond its true merit. But I felt it was my piece of art, just one degree from having sketched it myself.

Unfortunately, someone else felt a similar way. The bidding started at £5,000, and soon rose to £8,000, which was my absolute, 100 per cent limit. I raised my paddle again at £8,400. The person on the phone said something to the auction house staffer in the room, and the staffer relayed the news with a nod. £8,600. I bid £8,800. More phone talk. Another nod. The auctioneer looked at me with a look approaching pity, which I regarded as encouragement. My paddle said £9,000. Who *was* that person on the phone? Why did they want *Fish and Chip Shop* so much? After a few more back-and-forths I conceded defeat, and the auctioneer said 'It's yours!' to the faceless buyer at the end of the line. Worse was to come: the successful buyer's number – let's call it 666 – was logged several times in what remained of the sale. They were buying a lot of work. Perhaps they were speculating, perhaps they were decorating a loft. At any rate, I couldn't see how they could have loved the picture like I did.

The next time I saw another copy of the print was at the London Art Fair at Islington's Business Design Centre. A lot of fairs were held here regularly, including the bi-annual stamp show Stampex. Alan Cristea, one of the art galleries that had established itself in Cork Street following Kasmin's departure, took a regular stand at the London Art Fair, and displayed its crowd-pleasing array of Hodgkins and Opies and Blakes and Caulfields, and in 2002 it had a copy of *Fish and Chip Shop*. I saw the left half of it first, from an angle of about twenty yards. Then I got nearer, and saw the right side. There was a little red dot on the side of its frame that indicated it had been spoken for.

'Just sold it,' a man confirmed.

'When exactly?'

'Half an hour ago.'

'Half an hour ago? Really? Can I ask for how much?'

'It was ten thousand pounds. Are you familiar with it?'

'Yes, I almost bought it myself once.' Almost, I pondered. Could have, but didn't. 'I have a sentimental attachment to it.'

'It was one of his earliest works,' the helpful man said. 'Done when he was still at art school in Bradford. The boy being served is Hockney.'

A long gap. 'The thing is,' I said, noticing it was a full red dot rather than just a half one (which would have meant that the buyer had an option on it and was thinking it over for a while), 'is there any chance the buyer will change his or her mind?'

'No! They've just given me the cheque.'

The gallerist seemed upset that I was upset. He came up with what he thought was compensation.

'We do have *Woman with a Sewing Machine*, which is from the same period. I'm not sure I have it with me, though.'

I knew this work. It was a bit static, I thought. A flat-faced woman with high hair at her Singer.

'Thanks,' I said eventually. 'I'll keep on looking.'

This has been the case, and now the price has risen out of my league. If *Fish and Chip Shop* came up for auction today, it would probably be nudging £15,000. Because by the summer of 2007, only fifteen years after Kasmin and his colleagues had judged the art world to be in trouble, the art world wasn't in trouble any more. In fact, it had gone totally nuts, with ordinary art reaching ridiculous prices and the money flooding in from big City bonuses and Russia. So Kasmin's fears – he told me in 1992 that he thought he was seeing something far worse than a recession, something approaching meltdown – turned out to be unfounded. One of the beneficiaries of the boom fifteen years later was Kasmin's son Paul, who had become a big dealer in New York. Not that this helped me: my *Fish and Chip Shop* became more unaffordable every year; once, when Hockney made it more than fifty years ago, it was worth about twenty large portions of cod. When I first saw it, it was about a thousand portions, and now it could feed the entire population of Bridlington.

That was my first mature experience of object desire. As a child I had coveted toys and such, and of course some early error stamps, but as a child one has no easy method of obtaining something one desires beyond nagging or the upcoming birthday. We do not have credit cards or the possibility of the remortgage. But by the time I had started getting mad for stamps again when I turned forty, all that had changed. I had three credit cards and I began to hear voices in my head: Why would anyone pay £5,000 for a tiny bit of postage? And I began to answer: Because it is exceptionally good value.

The only other piece of art I had wanted as much as the Hockney was much cheaper. In theory. In practice, as David Brandon had told me, if it's not available then the price is immaterial.

As far as I could tell, Terry Frost had a few things in common with David Hockney. They were both popular artists fond of experimentation, they both made prints, they were both personally and creatively accessible. They both delighted in light and colour, they were both Royal Academicians, and they both smoked. In 1978, Frost started making bold ceramics – mugs and plates in limited editions and unlimited editions to be sold in the Tate and Royal Academy gift shops, and on one trip to St Ives with my wife in the late 1980s I bought four of the mugs from the back of a gallery – two red and black, two yellow and black. We got them home and started drinking out of them until one got broken and we decided they should be put on a shelf for display only. Then something tipped, and I decided that these mugs should form the basis of another collection. And so it was happening again, like it had happened before and would always happen: I wanted more of something I had never wanted before. Before the Internet, this collection would only be added to by subsequent trips to St Ives. Then I bought a couple of plates at auction. Then I bought a mug on eBay in 2001. I have five Frost plates, and seven Frost mugs, and to me they are stunning: bold, solid, sunburst. They brighten any room. There are two plate designs and two mug designs I don't have, and this wouldn't normally bother me; they'll turn up, I think, and their value is uncertain, and I may get a bargain. Unfortunately I have an adversary, an unexpected one; he is a dealer, a trader with Frost ceramics on display in his window, and he won't sell. Why won't he sell? I don't think it's money. I think it's personal.

He is a man called Henry Gilbert, known to his friends as Gillie, and he runs a shop in St Ives near the Barbara Hepworth Museum called Wills Lane Gallery. At least I like to think of it as a shop: you go in, he greets you, you look around, if you see something good and can afford it then you can buy it. This works for most things in the shop, but not the Frost ceramics. The reason for this may be gamesmanship – the unique power of the dealer over the collector – and it may lie deeply embedded in the creative history of St Ives, or at least from that point where Barbara Hepworth and Ben Nicholson came down during the war to live in nearby Carbis Bay and unleashed the wild and elemental area in stone and marble and carved relief and paint.

The reason why St Ives attracted Hepworth and Nicholson and later Rothko and Pollock was the same reason it had attracted holidaymakers and artists almost a century before: the remarkable Mediterranean light. For the tourists the light illuminated the beaches and the cottages set into the hillside, and for the artists it illuminated a new non-figurative way of imagining the natural world; no view was ever the same twice, as the granite, slate, heather, wind and sea created a space where the artist could quite realistically believe themselves to be part of the landscape rather than just a chronicler of it.

Gillie, who was an architect, came down and became a friend of the scene: not only Hepworth, but also Patrick Heron, Peter Lanyon, Roger Hilton, Naum Gabo, Wilhelmina Barns-Graham and the Leach family. He formed a close bond with two men in particular: John Wells, a doctor based on the Isles of Scilly who came relatively late to abstraction, and Terry Frost, who came to Cornwall in 1946 after four years as a prisoner of war. When Frost died in 2003 at the age of eighty-seven, Gillie (who I judged to be in his early eighties at the time, firmly established as the oldest and most anecdotal Trustee of Tate St Ives) set up a sunny shrine to his friend: some hand-made Christmas card collages Frost made each year, a couple of small prints, and some mugs and a plate. Every time I went in there – which was approximately every nine months – we would do the same dance.

'Hello Gillie, how are you?'

'Hello!'

Occasionally he didn't recognise me, but I didn't mind that. Usually I was just delighted to find him in. Often the lights were on, and it was regular trading hours, but Gillie was else-where, possibly in his inner sanctum, a little office at the far end which looked like it had been hit by jungle animals. Somewhere in that sanctum, perhaps on the floor, was a cheque of mine. I had given this to Gillie in exchange for a small paint-ing by the architect Ffiona Lewis, but as my bank statements came in each month the cheque failed to register. After six months the cheque became void, and perhaps it lay in the office with other cheques of a greater magnitude. I should have spread the word – Free Art! – but thought this would be bad karma, and Gillie's place was all about karma. I had been told that sometimes he wasn't in the gallery, and wasn't in the inner sanctum, but he had left the door open. Occasionally he would even leave it open at night, all those Christopher Wood paint-ings and white reliefs by Ben Nicholson in perspex cases, lean-ing up against William Scott pears and cups in their boxy white frames, and he would return the next day and everything would be exactly as it was. The shop was protected by angels, and the world loved Gillie; there was no more logical way of explaining it.

Whenever he was in, Gillie had a strong hand to play: the art of temptation. Our conversation usually proceeded in a predictable manner. He asked me what I did for a living. I said I was a writer – journalism and books. He spoke of the writers he knew.

'Have you seen the court building in Truro?' he would ask.

'I love it,' I would answer.

'It was designed by Evans and Shalev.'

'Who also did the Tate,' we'd say together.

Once I mentioned stamps, but it took a while to find the right way in. 'Terry Frost designed a stamp,' I said.

'Did he?'

'Well, actually no. He didn't design it, because it appeared in 2004, the year after he died. But they used one of his paintings, and one by Sonia Delauney, to illustrate the centenary of the Entente Cordiale. In a unique and symbolic move, France issued the same stamps, but in euros rather than pence. They almost caused a philatelic revolt, such was the dismay at the simplicity and childish nature of the design.'

'Did I tell you about my brother?' Gillie would ask.

'Yes. He went to the LSE.'

'That's right, he did go to the LSE.' He explained that he died.

'I went to the LSE too,' I'd say, to lighten the mood. 'Economic History. I met Veerasamy Ringadoo, the First President of Mauritius.'

'Did you know . . .' then a few names I hadn't heard of, followed by 'Do you ever go to the Alba?' This was a good fish restaurant on the harbour front.

'Once,' I said. 'It was delicious.' And then, running out of things to say, I said, 'Um, has Tate St Ives changed things much around here?'

We were obviously skirting around, waiting for the main event. Gillie sat in a brightly coloured plastic chair by the door as I looked around. Every time I went in there the good stuff was more depleted. When I started visiting in my late teens it was mostly original oils on boards, and the last time I went it was framed Andy Warhol posters. In recent years, many of Gillie's best works appeared in the London auctions and did well, especially works by John Wells, who was newly in demand. But the Frost mugs and plates hung around, occasionally moving from one window-sill to the other, leaving a soft ring of dust behind each time. I can't imagine I was the only one after them, but when I returned each time and found that they were still there it was with relief, and a certain satisfaction that Gillie had proved as stubborn with his other visitors. There was no price on them, just as there was no price on most of his works; the very good ones were priced in his head, and they probably swung wildly according to his mood. On one occasion I was in the shop when an American came in and saw a Barbara Hepworth print. These were not her key works, and you could snap up a fair one for a couple of grand.

'How much?' the American asked.

'Priceless,' Gillie said, unwilling to sell at ten times its market worth.

If he didn't like you he probably wouldn't even sell you a Warhol poster.

After another ten minutes of friendly but familiar conversation – had I seen the Hepworth outside the St Ives guildhall, had I been to her grave at Carbis Bay – I realised it was time to step up to the plate.

'How much for the plates?' I said. 'And the mugs?'

'They were designed by Terry Frost,' he would say.

'Yes. How much would you want for them?'

'They're not for sale at the moment,' Gillie replied. 'Terry died in 2003.'

'When do you think they will be for sale?' I doubted whether Count Ferrary ever had to pussyfoot around like this.

'In four months?' Gillie said, and the question mark was doom-laden.

'So if I came back in four months, I might be able to buy them?'

Nine months later, when I came down again, the mugs and plates would still be there, and their imminent departure would still be four months away.

'I'd be willing to pay a good price,' I'd say, hating myself as I did.

Gillie looked a bit offended. Clearly this wasn't about money any more. It was about art, and the truth about art was that some things were just not for sale.

I returned to St Ives in April 2007. I had prepared myself for the usual ordeal with Gillie, partly dreading it, half excited that this time I'd be successful. As I walked up to his gallery from the harbour, the path was blocked by workmen and their van. They were working at Gillie's gallery, and had already gutted it. Gillie was nowhere to be found, and all his pictures and ceramics were gone. 'We're refitting,' one of the workmen said. 'It's still going to be a gallery, but I don't think the old man is involved any more.'*

The next time I saw Hockney was at his studio in the Hollywood Hills. He was designing two things. The first was a poster for the Tate, and the other was a stamp depicting a scene in a Californian desert. We talked about his age, his dogs and his hearing. 'It's getting worse and worse,' he said, as he showed me the box controlling his new hearing aids. 'It's not silence you get – I like silence – but it's a din, a cacophony. My

* Gillie retired, and when he left his shop for the last time he took his plates with him.

father was the same; for the last ten years of his life he probably didn't hear a single word my mother said.'

And we talked about sex before AIDS. 'Oh, yeah. I spent a lot of time in New York in the late seventies and early eighties, working for the Metropolitan Opera. You could have sex with all kinds of people. If you had to organise that at home you'd have to have somebody professional to plan it.'

When we talked about stamps he said: 'The problem with stamps is that they are very small. Just when you think you have them licked, there's always another element to think of. Licked – do you get it? I thought that was quite funny actually.'

I told him about my regret at not buying the *Fish and Chip Shop* lithograph years before, and he said, 'Ah well, you see . . .' but then he trailed off and thought of something else. After years of experimentation with photo collage, photocopying and faxing, Hockney had recently rediscovered the joys of painting. He had completed a series of small portraits of friends and flowers and cacti, and the colour proofs of the catalogue for the London show of this work had arrived by FedEx that morning. These were rolled up uncut sheets, with half of the pages and illustrations printed upside down. He looked at them carefully, and took out a magnifying glass to examine certain details. Then he found a pen and started drawing on the proof, sketching and cross-stitching below several pictures so that it looked as though they were resting on easels. He drew lines on the edges of other illustrations, so that they resembled staples on the sides of taut canvas. Then he wrote, 'For Simon, David H,' and handed the proof to me.

Perforations

Stanley Gibbons celebrated its 150th anniversary in 2006, and the main thing the company appeared to be interested in that year was the possibility of stamps making you rich. The SG Investment Department was being quoted in the *FT* and on the BBC website, and it was printing lavish leaflets about portfolios and fixed-return contracts. It was a buoyant time for stamps, some of which had outstripped property inflation. The Gibbons leaflet asked the simple question – 'Why Invest in Stamps?' – and its unequivocal answers were designed to set any waverers with hedge funds and Christmas bonuses on a direct path to the Strand.

'Stamps are a $10 billion per annum global business,' the leaflet claimed, but it was an unsourced figure, alongside the statement that '30 million collectors worldwide protect price and liquidity'. Thirty million? Where were these people? Other reasons to invest in stamps were: 'Emerging markets: Russia, China and India; appreciation of national heritage; supply shortage and increasing demand; 50,000 people per month enter the over-fifties market in the UK (source: *FT*); the Internet is a key factor for recruitment and growth.'

According to Stanley Gibbons, the best place to invest in

stamps was Stanley Gibbons. It was the oldest stamp brand, if you didn't count the Post Office or the Queen's head; it has held a royal warrant since 1914; it claimed to have recruited ten times more new customers in 2004 than 1994 (many of them through the possibilities of the Internet). The company was offering three investment options. There was the big one, the Stamp Investment Fund, domiciled offshore, minimum investment £20,000 held for five years, stamps all with a minimum catalogue value of £1,000. Then there were the managed portfolios, more flexible, stamps all pre-1900, stored in a secure vault, flexible payment and investment period options. And finally there were fixed-return contracts, set between three and twenty years, with a minimum investment of £5,000 and a return of 5–7 per cent per annum. You could get these packages in a 'free guide', which had a heart-warming image on the front: a man with grey hair in glasses – presumably a dad – enthusiastically poring over a pile of stamp albums and catalogues while a cool-looking spiky-haired teenage boy – presumably his son – looked on appreciatively. It was a photo only an ad agency could put together, and it resembled a famous advert for the watchmaker Patek Phillipe, which also had a father and son combo: 'You never actually own a Patek Phillipe,' the strapline pronounced. 'You merely look after it for the next generation.' What a swizz. There should have been a similar line with the Gibbons photo: 'You will never actually get your cool and truculent MySpacing son anywhere near your stamp collection. Until the day he can offload it at an auction house.'

For a while in 2005, Stanley Gibbons and other stamp companies were also getting very excited about SIPPS, Gordon Brown's plan to allow stamps and other investments as part of a pension plan, with all the attendant tax breaks. This meant that collectors could buy some great items and claim 40 per cent from the Inland Revenue at the close of the financial year; they would obviously have to sell them again at retirement age, but at least they could enjoy them for a while. And then Gordon Brown realised that people would be buying all sorts of things they enjoyed, including holiday cottages, and he changed his mind.

But stamps were still being touted as a safe bet. In the 150th anniversary edition of *Gibbons Stamp Monthly*, Mike Hall, the company's chief executive, expounded on the beauty of compound returns on a long-term investment. At the Alternative Investment Show in 2004, Gibbons launched what it called its '30 Rarities Index', a collection of valuable stamps, most of them unused, dating from the 2d blue of 1840 to the 1903 10d dull purple and carmine 'official'. Fifty years earlier, these thirty stamps had a catalogue value of £8,360, and in 2004 this had increased to £861,000. Hall then extrapolated the current prices to the company's bicentennial in 2056. Based on previous performance, the stamps could be catalogued at more than £186 million, if anyone was still around who was interested in them. Reading this reminded me of the famous prediction from another century, a forecast that if the boom in horse-drawn carriages continued at the same crazy rate, the streets would soon be covered in nine feet of horseshit.

The first issue of *Gibbons Stamp Monthly* appeared in October 1927. Its first editorial spoke of stamps purely as 'the ideal recreation for hours of leisure'. The big concern some eighty years ago was not money but the two-pronged assault from radio and cinema, both perceived threats to contented evenings with hinges and tweezers. But no matter: the great hobby will prevail, for it promotes mental agility and individuality, and dedication brings a satisfaction far superior to the inanities of Americanised culture and the 'vacuous countenances' resulting from overexposure to the wireless. 'It is not strange, then,' the editorial suggested, 'that stamp collecting goes forward, while its competitors are largely static.'

Several dealers I spoke to, traditionalists all, said that Gibbons's bullish pecuniary approach made them nervous. Stamps were for pleasure, they maintained, and profit should be secondary. They began to sound like the advice I'd received as a boy: 'More rubbish has been written about the investment side of stamp collecting than perhaps any other side of the hobby,' I had been instructed in a pamphlet called *Let's Collect Stamps*. 'Anyone who wishes to make a pure and simple investment would do well to find something other than stamps into which to put his money.'

Most of the dealers I consulted had done rather well out of the stamps-as-investment line, and they knew that their clients didn't spend more than £10 on anything without the hope, however furtive, that one day they'd be able to sell at a profit. Accordingly, even the smaller dealers were establishing their own investment portfolios.

As usual, David Brandon presented a convincing case. In order to sell stamps to people who weren't stamp collectors he had to dismiss their common fears. The first of these was the concern that stamps were just little pieces of paper that had often been sent through the post. Collecting stamps appears to satisfy a natural human need, Brandon told them. 'Before international travel and television, it provided a link with an exotic and unknown world far away.' When stamp collecting began, people enjoyed getting stamps from places they would never see. These days, with international travel scattering collectors worldwide, people collect to keep in touch with their country of origin. 'The fact that collecting continues to be strong confirms that its foundations are rooted in a need that is not being satisfied by other means.'

Despite the fact that stamps only have a perceived value, they have an advantage over things such as Pez dispensers or Batmobiles: 170 years of history. Their value has been established in auction house catalogues, their provenance logged by collectors of discrimination.

One reason stamps are not a fad is because we live in a world full of horrors. 'For individuals with some accumulated wealth,' Brandon wrote, 'stamps represent a portable vehicle for flight should that become a necessity.' Stamps are easier to conceal across international borders than gold or diamonds. Jews fled Germany in the 1930s with stamps in their wallets, and they set a pattern for the wealthy refugee in decades to come.

Over lunch one day David Brandon told me that many of his non-collectors who had invested in stamps as an alternative to horses or football clubs had quickly become entranced by the few items in their portfolio, and in the course of learning more about them they had become specialists. Busy people also found them relaxing and transforming. I was reminded of a comment made by Richard Briers, the actor best known for his role in *The Good Life*. Briers had appeared in a television adaptation of a book I had written, and in the course of the filming I was pleased to learn of his interest in stamps. 'I'm one of those who looks at postmarks and things,' he said. 'It's a very calming thing to sort things out. You have a load of stamps and you sort them out into colours or prices or whatever. You're doing therapy. If you have a life of stress, like actors and most people do, it's very nice to have a quiet hobby. Leonard Rossiter died quite young because he was an extremely energised actor with an enormous amount of energy but unfortunately his hobby was squash. That is not good!'

But Briers was now in his seventies, and he made me think about what will happen to stamps in forty years, when so many of the current collectors have sold up or died. Where are the young collectors to take their place and buy their stamps to keep the market afloat? Could stamps go the way of music hall – good in their time, but finished off by the young world looking elsewhere for its amusement?

Possibly, but not just yet. After calling at the Brandons one day, and failing in my mission not to buy a stamp, I drove a few miles to the village of Mayford, near Woking, to visit the home of Richard Ashton. Ashton was the head of the stamp department at Sotheby's, and as I arrived he was laying out an auction catalogue of rare Australian stamps on his dining-room table. 'This is really exceptional,' he said, pointing to a particular strip. 'And this is probably the best example in the world . . .' It was the third sale of stamps from the collection of Sir Gawaine Baillie.

Baillie was the £11 million man, the former racing driver and engineer who had secretly amassed such an enormous and impressive collection of stamps that it would take Sotheby's ten sales and two years to sell them all.* The vast sale catalogues were magnificent achievements in themselves, a lavish and educational guide to many of the world's most valuable stamps. To the average collector it was unimaginable that one man could have collected so many fine items, particularly since Baillie did not become serious about collecting until middle age.

'When you've met so many collectors you get a feeling for how serious they are going to be,' Richard Ashton told me. When Baillie first turned up at Sotheby's to a public viewing of

* The ten sales were so significant that when they were complete in January 2007, Sotheby's decided to hold another sale entitled 'Missed Opportunities', more than four hundred pages of items that failed to sell first time around. A quarter of the proceeds would go to the London Clinic Liver Centre, as Sir Gawaine's widow, Lady Baillie, had received a liver transplant in 2006.

a forthcoming sale, Ashton invited him upstairs to have a private view. This set a pattern. 'Whenever we had sales, I met him for an early breakfast at about 7.15 at the café opposite Sotheby's back door in George Street. He'd then come up, and his viewing would be over by the time any of the staff arrived.' Baillie would then send his bids in, and the auctioneer would act on his behalf. He attended very few sales in person. 'I think he knew that if he sat in an auction and spent £20,000 on a stamp, every dealer in the country would be on to him.'

Although Baillie kept careful records of every purchase, a prospective bidder for one of his items would have no idea of how much he paid and how much the stamp had accrued in value. In the first Baillie sale of Great Britain, the catalogue of which I had pored over for hours and learnt almost by heart, there were at least twenty classic errors I would have been proud to own. The stamp I wanted from him most, the 1961 1s 3d Parliamentary, had probably been bought from David and Mark Brandon many years before, and soon I would have to compete with them at the auction to ensure they didn't buy it back. Richard Ashton knew the Brandons well, along with the other error collectors I would now have to regard as my opposition, and although he was a traditionalist he understood the appeal of missing colours and Queen's heads. He showed me some nice errors in the draft Australian catalogue on his desk, and then he told me about the time a woman came into his place of work with an item he had never seen before.

In 1963, when he was still in his teens, Ashton was working at Harmer Rooke, an auction company owned by Stanley Gibbons. A nervous young woman was at the front desk of his office in Arundel Street, near the Strand. She said she had just bought a sheet of stamps from the post office and there was something wrong with them. When she took them out of her bag she showed Richard Ashton a set of British stamps commemorating the opening of the Trans-Pacific Cable (COMPAC: COMmonwealth PACific Cable). Almost nine million were sold, but in the central panel of this particular sheet, twenty-four of them were missing black, which meant the word 'Commonwealth' and the cable running around a blue globe weren't there. A senior buyer from Stanley Gibbons arrived within a few minutes to make her an offer. 'I can't remember how much,' Ashton says, 'but I do remember catching her on the way down as she fainted.' Gibbons exhibited the sheet at a big stamp show, and then sold it for £600; in 2006, just one of the twenty-four sold at auction for more than £3,000.

Ashton, an owlish and affable man, did not grow up with stamps. He was born just after the Second World War. His parents had arrived in England penniless from the Channel Islands, while others in his family had been interned in Germany. His father was keen for his son to become an engineer, but after a day-release visit to Dagenham Motor Works from his technical college, Richard realised his calling lay elsewhere. He replied to an advert in a London evening paper for a trainee accountant, and the firm that answered was Stanley Gibbons. Inevitably, Ashton had collected stamps as a child, but his knowledge was limited. When, during his job interview, he was asked how he would detect a watermark on a stamp, his prospective employers were probably expecting an answer involving benzene and a tray. Ashton said he would hold the stamp up to a light, which is exceptionally ineffective. But he got the job, and started working at Harmer Rooke. He soon moved away from accounts to work in the stamp room, and found he had a photographic memory.

After sixteen years with Gibbons, Ashton moved to Sotheby's. Sotheby's held its first big stamp auction in 1872, and sales continued until the First World War, but were discontinued when one of its experts failed to return at the end of it. It was decided to relaunch the philatelic department in the 1970s, and Ashton slowly worked his way up. His big moment came in 1982, when word reached him that Sir Maxwell Joseph wished to sell his collection of Cape of Good Hope. Ashton's eyes began to water as he told me the tale.

And my eyes lit up. My father had once represented Sir Maxwell in a minor legal matter. It was big news at our house. Sir Maxwell was the sole owner and proprietor of Grand Metropolitan Hotels, and rarely a day went by when he didn't appear in the *Evening Standard* business section. He started collecting Cape of Good Hope for the same reason that most young people do – the unusual triangular shape. He then branched out to pre-stamp postal history going back to the Dutch settlement, and then to the end of the Boer War and the Siege of Mafeking. 'He would buy individual items at auctions, but like Count Ferrary he'd much prefer to infuriate his rivals by buying complete collections. It was a surprise when he decided to sell up.' Ashton only found out what lay behind his decision shortly before the sale.*

Sotheby's had to bid for the honour of hosting the auction.

---

* There are many reasons why stamp collecting is not the thing it was for the young, and one of them may be the decline of the traditional family. If parents and grandparents won't enthuse about philately, who will? Schools once did but don't any more. There are no philatelist footballers, few philatelist film stars (and if there are, they won't talk about it. What an image-crusher; Hollywood child-molesters stand more chance of rehabilitation).

A father and grandfather may be keen on stamps, but the children aren't, just as they aren't much interested in carrying on the family business these days. In this way the stamps leave the family, and find their way to dealers and auctions. The case of Sir Maxwell Joseph represented no finer example of this.

Its principal rival was a one-man philatelic industry called Robson Lowe, a grand old patriarch of British stamps who knew more stamp people, and had seen more stamp things, and wrote more articles and books than any other. He also ran an auction house, and Richard Ashton knew it would be a challenge to persuade Sir Maxwell Joseph not to go with him. So before he and his Sotheby's colleagues went to see him in his office in Oxford Street they came up with an interesting proposal.

'I was terrified,' Ashton recalls. 'He was sitting behind this huge desk, and he sat back and said, "Well, you better tell me how you're going to sell my collection."' The Sotheby's people said that for maximum impact they proposed to offer it as one single sale, about a thousand lots over three days. Robson Lowe had told him it would be four or five auctions. Sotheby's also proposed issuing a hardback catalogue, something it had only done about half a dozen times before.

Sir Maxwell thought this was a novel approach, but then posed the inevitable question: 'What are you going to charge me?' This was the clincher; an average vendor's commission was 15 per cent, although this would decrease for a major sale. The Sotheby's team said, 'After the auction you pay us the commission that you think we've earned.' Richard Ashton remembers Joseph looking straight at him as he said, 'Done.'

Then they asked him why he was selling. 'Put it this way,' he answered. 'If the day should come when I die, I've got three children, and I don't want them falling out over my stamp collection. It's indivisible, but the money from it can be split three ways.' This was the same reason offered by Geoff Hurst when he was asked why he was selling the shirt he wore when he scored the hat-trick in the World Cup Final: he had three daughters and how on earth would they split the shirt when he died? Sir Maxwell didn't tell Ashton that he had already been diagnosed with terminal cancer.

Unfortunately, Sir Maxwell died a month before his sale. In the few months between striking the deal and the design of the catalogue, his cancer had spread. He was confined to bed for much of the time that Ashton was pricing the estimates for each lot, and he died on the day the catalogue was published. Ashton sent a copy to him at home, and he heard from Lady Joseph that he did get to see it.

In the weeks before the auction, Sotheby's received a lot of criticism for selling the entire collection in one go, rather than spread over a year; buyers will be overwhelmed, people said, and run out of money. But Sotheby's sold every lot, one of the few sales at the auction house that fetched over £1 million. The Lear-like disposal of the collection had given his daughters financial security, and philatelists throughout the world had gained from the dispersal. But Ashton's celebrations were muted, for he still had to see Sir Maxwell's executors about the commission; they were not stamp people, and contractually they owed Sotheby's nothing. But they liked the boldness of the existing arrangement, and they offered a handsome percentage. Ashton told me Sotheby's probably would have settled for no commission at all, being satisfied with the buyer's premium alone and the great privilege of selling one of the greatest collections ever assembled.

After that, many other fine sales followed, but none rivalled the immense challenge and privilege of curating the Baillie collection. Lady Baillie thought it might be worth £800,000 rather than the £11 million Sotheby's estimated. Dealers – there may have been about thirty Baillie bought from regularly – were equally surprised, as many thought they were his main suppliers.

Ashton first met Baillie around the time of the Sir Maxwell Joseph sale, and he began to think of him as a friend as well as a client. He was deeply saddened when he died at the end of 2003, and he was keen to ensure that his stamps were handled well. All the big auction houses have staff employed primarily to keep track of the changing fortunes of great collectors. Obituaries are studied carefully; contacts are pursued among divorce lawyers. Richard Ashton confirmed the benefit of a subtle approach: Is there anything we can do to help? 'It sounds rather macabre,' he told me, 'but if you don't do it, someone else will.'

But before Sotheby's competed to handle the Baillie sale, he was called in for a probate valuation. He was astounded. 'It didn't matter which book I picked up,' he remembered, 'every one was a gem. There were items I remembered from auctions twenty years ago and didn't know who had bought them, and there they were.' Ashton told Lady Baillie that Sotheby's were going to show people what a wonderful accomplishment it was that her husband had formed this great collection. The catalogues would end up being a memorial to him. Lady Baillie said, 'the wider the distribution the better'.

And so here, on 1 October 2004, was my chance.

The 1961 1s 3d Green Parliamentary Conference without the blue Queen's head. Baillie's example consisted of a progressive row of three stamps (the first perfect with the blue present, the second with the blue half-gone, the third with the blue gone altogether), and the estimate on it appeared to me to be quite reasonable. I could afford even the top estimate of £2,500 plus a buyer's premium of 17.5 per cent. I doubted that anyone could be as determined to buy it as I was. A total of 5,760,000 were printed in their perfect form, six were imperfect, and now there was a once-in-a-lifetime opportunity for me to realise an ambition.

I set two alarms on the morning of the sale, even though it began at 10.30 and my lot probably wouldn't be on the block until 1 p.m. I didn't tell anyone where I was going. I had three credit cards in my pocket. I arrived early and signed up for a bidding paddle, but there was a lot of other business to be got through before the QE2 errors, including many fine blocks of George V Seahorses, the stamps that had done for me in the school stamp competition. This was a bad omen, and not the only one in the saleroom that morning. Many of the hundred or so other people present, far more experienced than me, were startled at the steep prices that many of the lots were reaching, some of them twice or three times the upper estimate. Several dealers I knew spent much of the morning tutting and shaking their heads. This was a terrible indication.

The two major QE2 errors before mine each went very high. The Post Office Savings Bank without black attained £13,000, £4,000 more than the upper estimate, while the European Postal and Telecommunications Conference strip, in which the green dove erroneously turned white, went for £6,000, more than three times the estimate, to a bidder on the phone.

And now it was my turn. I knew that the £2,000–£2,500 estimate was going to be much too low. I thought I could afford £6,000.

The bidding began slowly. After a few bids we were at £4,000 and the interest seemed to be petering out. I thought to myself, 'I'm going to be okay.' I put up my paddle. The auctioneer said, '£5,000, new bidder.' For a moment there was silence. This was going to be a great day for me.

Then a white-haired woman at the very front, seated by a desk, said '£10,500'. I knew who the woman was. It was Mary Weekes, a stamp agent acting on behalf of anonymous clients. Her bid of £10,500 was the amount she had needed to clear the under-bidder. I may have imagined it, but I think that at that moment a movie cliché happened in the saleroom: there was collective sucking-in of breath. And then the gavel came down and I felt empty inside, like an amateur who has just discovered hidden rules in a professional game.

I'd failed to buy my favourite stamp and I might never have the chance again.

And yet what had I missed and what had I saved?

The answer to the first: a small piece of paper, gummed on one side, produced in 1961 at the printing works of Harrison & Sons of London and High Wycombe, Buckinghamshire, whose machinery had for one second run out of blue ink.

The answer to the second: about £6,000, the price I was prepared to bid up to, roughly three times the estimate.

Rationally, financially, a good outcome. Yet I was morose for a week. I would have been elated to have got it, but also guilty at having spent so much. So there was a problem: stamps were no longer making me happy.

The Error World

I have decided to sell my stamps. This could be an error. Unfortunately, I have little choice.

Everyone has their own story of how they fell out of love with stamps, and many can remember the exact date. For some it was 13 February 2001, the day picture stamps went self-adhesive. Not for me. I've always been a great fan of pictures of dogs in baths and cats in shoulder-bags, and the set that appeared on 13 February was satisfying. There was a dog in a bath, a cat in a bag, a dog on a bench and a cat in a sink, all black and white and arty, ten first-class stamps in a booklet that you peeled off and applied like sticking plaster. They made me wonder what had taken Royal Mail so long to get its act together.

Some years earlier, the Penny Black had used its 'cement' to keep it attached to envelopes. Removing it was rather easy, as it wasn't very sticky and its application was thin. One reason for the rapidly inflated price of the Penny Black to collectors, apart from the fact that it was the first in the catalogue and every collector had to have one, was because so many of them never made it to their destinations, dropping off in transit – mail-coaches, mailbags, sorting depots – and swept away a few days later. The adhesive dried out and cracked easily, it tasted foul, and its varying colour – from off-white to light brown – hinted at the inconsistency of its manufacture. The adhesive, known as 'British gum', was applied by hand with a brush. It was made from potato and wheat starch heated to 400 degrees Fahrenheit, and after a few years the recipe was enhanced by bovine gelatin and two coats were applied. Not long after the appearance of the Penny Black, the story arose that licking the gum gave you cancer of the tongue, and in 1852 a Select Committee felt obliged to scotch the rumour by listing its ingredients, whereupon Charles Dickens wrote an essay in *Household Words* entitled 'The Great British Gum Secret'. From 1847 gum arabic – the sap of acacia trees grown in the Sudan and Nigeria – was sometimes used as a substitute, and applied to the stamp before printing, which often resulted in the stamps being printed on the gummed side, and thus failing to stick at all.

Before the cats and dogs appeared in 2001, the popular adhesive was polyvinyl alcohol gum, a chemical formulation coated by machine, often with an additional anti-bacterial agent. This pleased vegetarians, who could now lick without remorse. When I was young, my mother would discourage the licking of stamps the way she would discourage the eating of the cone part of ice-cream cones: just too much human dirt. I never had cause to lick many stamps in succession, and when I helped my parents with their party invitations or charity mailings I learnt how to dip my fingers into a small glass dish of water and then wet the stamps. I longed for one of those dampened sponge rings they had in post offices, but they were probably limited to industrial use. Whenever my maternal grandmother kissed me pungently on the cheek, which happened much too often (she would kiss me, but also have a small handkerchief ready to wipe it off, as if she were spraying and cleaning a vanity mirror), my mother would always say, 'You could lick a whole book of Green Shield Stamps with that!' Irreversibly dry in all other ducts and crevices, she generated enough saliva to cool Mount Etna.

Up until December 2005, I had never, as far as I can remember, been kissed passionately on my neck. But when it finally happened I felt my world ignite and fall apart at once, and I began an affair with a woman from my past, and my marriage of eighteen years dissolved. Within a year many things that I had never had to think about before came into focus. I had to find a new place to live, a new car, a whole new way of life. I had to forge new relationships with my children and friends. And I had to sell my stamps.

When I first met Richard Ashton and he mentioned the Three Ds – death, debt, divorce – that kept the auction houses going, I didn't think that any of them would apply to me for quite a while. But a few months later two of them had become a reality, and there I was with my errors, totalling up.

Several times during this period I looked at my stamps in a new way. I began to question again why I collect at all. What was the thread that tied my love of stamps and Costello and Tube maps and Chelsea badges? Perhaps it was a birth defect, or a disease acquired when young. I had been keeping myself well by fulfilling a physiological need, much as my youngest son Jake injected insulin for his diabetes. There is no use asking, 'Why me?'; a gene mutates and you just have to get on with it. There was little evidence of a genetic inheritance from my parents, but sometimes it just skips a generation: my maternal grandfather, a dentist, collected teeth and dental impressions (all dentists did this to some extent, but he went beyond, taking them home and displaying them to guests after dinner in glass cases).

Jean Baudrillard has observed that 'what you really collect is always yourself', and sometimes this makes vague sense to me – these were the things I loved, and I wanted to surround myself with them. And sometimes Baudrillard's comment explains the whole story – afraid of losing things, I wanted to hold everything close, to say 'this is mine, this rare thing. You will not take it from me until I see fit.' It had much to do with safety and security, which also explains the great importance I placed on protection and albums and cabinets.

At ground level we are all collectors. We satisfy our thirsts and hungers in literal ways – the shopping lists add to our food stores, our wardrobes house this season's collections. When we travel we gather passport stamps and photographs and stories. At work we collect contacts and experience. Freud classified three collections beyond his antiquities: his case histories, his dream texts and analyses, his Jewish anecdotes laden with world-weary lessons and wisdom. If we maintain a diary or a blog we want to remember or be remembered, and we offer up a collection of events and opinions that record diversity.

In 2006, during a sort-out necessitated by my divorce, I came across some boxes of photographs and documents that justified all my basest instincts as a collector, and confirmed the value of hoarding as well. I had seen most of the items in the boxes before: photographs in albums and loose, stretching back to my great-grandparents in Hamburg. There were photographs of my parents when they were babies in absurd white ruffled blouses supplied by the photographer, an image of my father in his army uniform, a photo of my mother, on her first day at school, carrying a cardboard cone of sweets almost as big as her. There's one of me in a pram being pushed by my brother. My first dog Gus, a holiday in Torquay with my mother and brother and my mother's arm over my shoulder, an outing to Cambridge, playing in the garden with a beach-ball – all the usual moving things, ordinary compared to what I uncovered next. These were documents from Germany, banking and employment papers, my parents' school reports, naturalisation papers, my mother's CV when she was working at a museum in Palestine, my father's army commendations and speeches on legal affairs.

And then there was one thing I couldn't remember seeing before. It is written on ten sides of thin white card, each the size of a piece of Wonderloaf. This is my mother's death diary, written by her home nurse during her last weeks with breast cancer from October to December 1979. It begins with a brief five-year medical history, a list of drugs taken, and a bit about me at the LSE at the age of nineteen (' . . . seldom home during the daytime, but is usually home in the evenings and is able to help prepare Mum some supper if she isn't feeling up to getting herself some').

It's an account of slow decline, and I'm not quite sure who it was written for; perhaps it was for another nurse taking over; perhaps it was for me. It was too painful to consider at the time, and I must have just put it in a document album and hoped I could look at it in years to come.

Friday, 26th October 1979: Over the worst of the high temperature. However, still feeling weak and unable to stay up for more than a few minutes.

Monday, 29th October: Cooked her own lunch today. Got up + dressed as friends calling in late afternoon.

Friday, 2nd November: Bathed, dressed, had lunch and went to have hair cut and set. Intends ringing GP as new batch of prednisolone is not enteric coated like the last. Not sure if it matters!

Wednesday, 7th November: Had arranged for friend to take her into Selfridges to try and buy a suitable wig. However, had to put this off as she felt she just couldn't make it.

Sunday, 23rd December: Decided to be up and about a bit. Mixed some matzo balls at the table in bedroom, then came downstairs and sat at stove and cooked them . . . Could hardly make it up the stairs again (had Simon and I on either side of her).

She died at the Middlesex Hospital six days later.

The more I considered my parents, the more I was able to acknowledge that stamps were compensating for something. The period of greatest involvement and expenditure on errors coincided with the strongest feelings of grief over the loss of my family. It was a somewhat delayed bereavement, but I understand that a delay of twenty-five years is not uncommon. My sessions at marriage guidance, at which we discussed the break-up of my present family, brought events into focus.

The sessions also made me think about something I rarely confronted. Or rather, someone. About eighteen months before she died, my mother went into remission. There seemed to be hope of a full recovery, the chemotherapy drugs pulling her through against the odds. She started making long-term plans again, and travelling to Israel to meet a man she had been friendly with for a while. My brother and I couldn't have been more delighted or surprised.

My brother Jonathan had recently qualified as a doctor, and was training to be a surgeon. In 1978, I was eighteen and he was twenty-three, and although the age gap was still considerable, his work at the Royal Free Hospital in Belsize Park meant that he still lived at home and we saw a good deal of each other.

He had a girlfriend called Jenny, also a medic, and their relationship was getting serious, and sometimes she stayed the night. I can't remember anything of our conversations, but he did help me with my A levels and my university applications. We played ping-pong on a makeshift table in his room, which was much larger than mine and had a lovely view of the garden, and we exchanged favourite records and cassettes. He was impressed that I had championed 'Jilted John' by Jilted John several weeks before it became a hit. And we both loved *All Mod Cons* by The Jam.

Three days after Christmas, which we barely celebrated, Jonathan returned from the hospital with a cold. He went to bed early, by himself. The next morning, I remember my mother calling him from the landing, but there was no reply. She knocked on the door and called again, but still nothing. This was not like him to sleep so long. The door was locked. My mother began to panic, and I didn't know what to think. I can't remember how his door was broken down. My mother found him dead, in bed.

The next week is a blank. I remember going to the funeral, and I've been told that one morning I came down to breakfast to find my mother sitting at the table with a knife in her hands. She was repeating two words: 'Why Jonathan? Why Jonathan? Why Jonathan?'

And after that I think she gave up, and her cancer took hold once more.

How did I react to my brother's death? Not well, and not badly. In the main, I blocked it out as best I could. Since then I have thought about Jonathan often, but I still find it difficult to talk about him. He died of viral pneumonia, which is usually only fatal in the very young or very old. It may be that his immune system was depleted by another infection he picked up at the hospital. In the past I have thought that he might have committed suicide, and I considered his locked door, but this thought has never made much sense to me.

He was a gentle, generous and loving young man, and very gifted. Had he lived, he would have saved a lot of lives. I suppose I coped with his death by writing a book about AIDS fifteen years later, a book partly concerned with medicine but principally with young men dying. And I coped with it by falling deeper into my passions.

My first serious relationship with a girl broke up around this time, and then university beckoned, and Elvis Costello, and other relationships, and a shot at student journalism. The one constant was stamps. Everything else in turmoil and flux, but the mail didn't let you down. New issues every few weeks, squirrelled away upstairs, and new discoveries at the dealers' windows. You can really bury your head in an album.

Some things stay the same. I began to lose interest in stamps when I was twenty, about a year after my mother died. The world was just too full of other things and new emotions, and I had learnt to distrust old alliances. I felt that stamps belonged only to my family childhood. Now I was an adult on my own, and I had come to deal with my bereavements by believing that there was no point dwelling on the past. Along with so much else, stamps were nothing but the past.

It was during a later period in my life, when things weren't going so well at home, that stamps again became all-consuming. Now it was our marriage that was dying. I once had ISAs and Tessas, but once those were spent on a new kitchen I decided to spend spare money on stamps instead. I was providing for my own family, but I also felt good about spending some of my earnings on my hobby, even though the sums involved – hundreds, occasionally thousands, on a stamp or block – were far greater than anything I would have spent a decade before. At one auction I spent just over £4,000 on several items, something I couldn't possibly admit to when I got home, no matter how excited I was. I went upstairs, looked at my new stamps, and put them away in my errors album, which I kept at the base of a built-in wardrobe in my office (a converted loft, initially an au pair's room).

Then I thought about what had just happened. A catalogue had arrived containing one man's stamps. But before that: a man had died and his widow had decided to sell his collection, something he had spent a great many hours with, something he may have cared about almost as much as life itself, if for no other reason than it gave his life order and meaning; this was probably something his wife couldn't understand no matter how much she tried or loved him. And before that: another man had a comparable passion, and had treasured and protected some nice items for the collectors who came next. It was a virtuous circle.

When I had failed to buy my favourite stamp error at the Baillie sale, it was only money that had robbed me of my chance to own something I wanted, but I felt downcast. But after a while the memory of disappointment fades. Losing a stamp at an auction does not send you off with a shrug to another hobby. Instead, it sends you deeper into stamps, consistently in search of satisfaction.

After the sale I made another call on Richard Ashton, and he consoled me with a tale of losing an item he thought should have been his. It was a ticket for the last ship to leave Guernsey before the Germans bombed the harbour. It was in a postal auction, and he bid six times the estimate but still didn't get it. 'I was so annoyed,' he told me. 'It was the boat my father was on.'

In the autumn of 2005 there was to be another Baillie sale of GB items. Ashton couldn't remember exactly what was to be in it, although he knew that there were no more 1s 3d Parliamentary stamps. He thought it would contain some more missing minis or Jaguars, and the largest existing block of missing Post Office Towers. He sent me an email which touched me more than any other communication I have ever received about stamps. He wrote that after the next Baillie GB catalogue was published, perhaps I'd like to come for a spot of lunch at Sotheby's and enjoy a private view.

But things were changing for me. In 2005, I had already begun to sense that my desire to acquire more stamps was waning. I began to feel uneasy with the secretiveness of it. This was not only the money I was spending on it and the secluded time with albums and catalogues, but also the fact that I couldn't easily display what I owned. Outside public exhibitions, it makes no sense to put stamps on display. They would be damaged by light, but there was a deeper problem: who, beyond other collectors, would appreciate them? I found it quite damaging when, on the rare occasions, when I would show people my stamps, they would show no interest. They didn't know what they were looking at, I couldn't adequately explain it, and I hurriedly put the albums back in the slipcases. I feel as I do when I describe the idea for a new book: it's complete in my head, but every time I talk about it it becomes diluted.

I also had a feeling that my error collection contained almost everything it ever would. It was an above-average collection, with some fine items in there, but it wasn't really going anywhere, or certainly not at the pace it had when I began it.

I wasn't interested in the less dramatic errors, the tiny flaws undetectable without a magnifying glass. And the more spectacular ones, the ones with only five or six prime copies, I couldn't afford. So my collection was just sitting there, less a living thing than a mausoleum. In addition, I had read a comment from Hilary Rubenstein, a clinical psychologist and Cochair of Junior Associates of the Museum of Modern Art, New York, in which she began to describe a condition I was edging towards. 'The urge to collect only becomes pathological or perverse for collectors when they really can't get any satisfaction from it. If their central experience is that they can't get enough and someone else always has more and they are always unhappy and envious and driving themselves to financial ruin, then that doesn't work out quite so well.'*

When my affair began at the end of 2005 I had another thing to keep hidden from the light. But it also made me question where I had been placing my affections. Freud was right – collecting as a substitute for sex. Even the loveliest of objects don't offer passion back. It made me go all Lennonish and wonder whether I could survive quite happily without any possessions at all, because now there was something else that filled the space previously satisfied, however briefly, by the desire for and purchase of objects. (The nature of stamp collecting is partly non-consumerist, as we safeguard artefacts that previously would have been used up and thrown away, but in the twenty-first century collecting ultimately always means buying things.) And so I imagined myself as George Eliot's Silas Marner, obsessing over his coin collection ('But at night came his revelry . . . He spread them out in heaps and bathed his hands in them . . . He handled them, he

* Quoted in *Owning Art: the Contemporary Art Collector's Handbook*, by Louisa Buck and Judith Greer, Cultureshock Media, 2006.

counted them, till their form and colour were like the satisfaction of a thirst to him . . .'), until his love of humanity and the living world is rekindled by his emotions towards the golden-haired child Effie.

Once I had decided to sell my errors, I had two options. The Brandons or an auction house. I called David Brandon to say I was thinking of selling, and he sounded interested. He asked me to send him digital photographs of the best items by email. The following day, after some very long downloads, he invited me down for another lunch. Perhaps, I thought, this would be the last time I would see him.

No sooner had I arrived at his house near Guildford than the phone rang in his office.

'Oh Harry, hello!' he said. Followed by, 'Oh . . . it's Danny! Even better! How are you, Danny? Good. Hmm . . . mmm. Probably yes, but I normally know the moment I see them if there's going to be a problem. I'll look at them, and if there's anything wrong I'll report it immediately. If not I'll put them in the back of my safe and sort them out in the months to come. It's not normally a question of forgery with your stuff, it's just a question of condition. Perhaps the odd tear or thin, which of course makes all the difference . . . I'll only tell you if there's a problem, and I'll simply say, "Lot number so-and-so will be returned because of this . . .", but I'm sure they'll all be all right. Yes. All the best, Danny, bye.'

'That was Danny,' Brandon said. 'I'm buying stuff all over the world.'

I asked whether his son Mark had spent a lot at the world convention in Washington.

'Absolute fortunes! And Linda was in London today, and she picked up from Grosvenor [an auction house], that was

£77,000 something. Then she went on to Spink [another auction house], that was £40-something thousand. It never stops . . . Right, we better have a look at your little bits and pieces.'

I opened my album.

Brandon said, 'I did do some work on it yesterday, and these are my notes, so let's hope that my notes are correct, the best notes I could do looking at your pictures. Do you want something to look at for five minutes? Do you want a car magazine?'

'Sure.'

'I just need to see if any of them are creased.'

'All of them are creased,' I said. 'I creased them all on the way down on purpose.'

'Let's have a look . . . the thing is, I'm buying very heavily at the moment and not selling very much.'

This was all classic Brandon. He once showed me his slippers – ghastly leatherette held together with tape – as an indication of how cash-strapped he was.

Linda arrived with the tea. 'Do you want your sandwich in here?' she asked.

'I think it will be safer in the kitchen,' Brandon suggested as he started cataloguing my stamps. 'Right, now where's my tweezers?'

Linda, from the hallway: 'Let me ask, do you want salad cream on it?'

Me: 'No thanks!'

Brandon: 'Don't have it too thick, Linda, just ordinary salmon, but not too thick or it will fall all over the place.'

Brandon turned back to my album, and I assumed nonchalance.

'So let's see if I've catalogued these correctly . . . in fact, if you want a job, if I call out the catalogue values, you write them down. Shouldn't take very long this . . . six times of these, that's

£800, that's . . . the tubes omitted in normal, £300 each, they've shot up . . . the World Cup . . . £800 . . . hmmmm . . . is this World Cup missing something? . . . ah, black omitted, £110 . . . and the Post Office Towers, £4,000.'

Brandon's plan was to offer me a good percentage of the values in the current Stanley Gibbons catalogue. Traditionally, the Gibbons prices were far higher than those charged by other dealers, and usually more than auction prices. But with errors, especially the rare ones, auction prices often matched the Gibbons catalogue and occasionally exceeded it.

'So that's £1,500, The Forth Bridge is £2,700, the Geographical with 4d value omitted, that's £160 each . . .'

And so it went on, through fifteen items. I felt a combination of sadness (that it had come to this, after years of collecting, my album on a dealer's desk being not admired but valued) and relief (that my stamps were indeed valuable, that I hadn't been buying rubbish, that the tiny pieces of paper had in many cases increased considerably in worth from the time I bought them; better still, Brandon was now valuing them at a greater price than he had sold them to me, which is a collector's dream. This very rarely happens).

And then there was more sadness. I would – by auction or Brandon – soon be saying goodbye to these coveted secret passions. Like a station-platform parting, part of me wanted to get it over with as quickly as possible. I didn't explain to him precisely why I had to sell – renting a flat, maintenance, buying a new car – but I'm sure he guessed, because he would have done this sort of thing many times before.

'The 1s 3d – did I sell you that? No? £1,600. It's amazing how some of these have gone up . . . the Ships missing red, £50 . . . the missing Queen's head, that's £280, then we've got the horsey, what year's the horsey?'

I consulted the catalogue. The horsey, a stamp featuring a painting by George Stubbs, was from 1967.

'You've got some nice stuff, Simon,' he said. 'I should know – I sold you a lot of it. At some point we probably owned 80–90 per cent of it.'

'Yes, a lot of it may be coming home.'

We talked about the amount we'd both save on commission charges if I sold to him rather than at auction. I'd save between 10 and 15 per cent seller's commission, and he'd save around 20 per cent including VAT. He argued that he could offer me more as a result, because when he's bidding at auction for my stamps he'd offer less, knowing that he'd have to add on 20 per cent at the end to the auction house. 'Auction is a place to buy, not to sell,' he told me several times. He claimed that I'd be the beneficiary, but I couldn't help thinking the big winner would always be him, the dealer. In the end, Brandon came up with a figure that I considered too low, so we haggled for a bit.

Then Brandon said he had something to show me that probably wouldn't mean a thing but excited him a great deal. As he opened his safe he said that what he was about to produce 'is much rarer than the stuff you've got, but the same period. Are you sitting down? I'm almost frightened to show you, because you'll become uncontrollable.'

There were several turns and clicks to the left and right before he removed two large envelopes. 'Look at that. Flowers from the endangered rainforest.'

I asked him what I was supposed to be getting excited about.

'This is 1960-something. Nineteen sixty-five I think. Singapore. There are probably only two sheets, and here's one of them.'

The sheet was missing a colour.

'It cost me an absolute fortune!' Brandon said. 'But I've got something even better. Do not move.' He stretched inside his safe again. 'You've heard of the Holy Grail, haven't you?'

He took out another sheet of flowers, with another spectacular missing colour.

'I may never sell it. If you look in here, Simon,' he said, motioning to the shelves in his safe, 'these are all my purchases over the last year yet to be sorted. I can barely get them all in there. And I've got another safe-ful next door.'

He showed me his Coutts cheque book. It was almost all stubs. There were two cheques left, and one of them could be for me if I wanted it. We left the price dangling. He said, with his pen poised, 'Christmas has come early for you!' And then we went for lunch.

A week earlier I had gone to see a man called Richard Watkins at Spink. Spink was established in 1666 as a goldsmith's and pawnbroker's. A century later it had a reputation as a leading coin dealer, and by 1900 it was satisfying a collectors' demand for medals. But Spink has only been auctioning stamps since 1997, when it bought the philatelic department of Christie's (formerly Robson Lowe). I had driven past its offices in Southampton Row perhaps five hundred times on my way through Holborn to the Aldwych and Waterloo. I had often wondered what went on there.

This was probably the fifth time I had visited. On three of those occasions I was a consumer, attending auctions and buying errors. Once I had gone as a journalist to talk about the nature of collecting, and now I was there as a prospective seller. On a previous visit I noticed that the ground floor was being remodelled to make it look more like a shop. You couldn't buy much apart from catalogues, but you could browse delicately lit glass cases displaying items from upcoming auctions. When I visited again a few months later, the developments were complete, and it was like walking into a Mayfair jeweller's. The stamps on show seemed even more special, and even more desirable. It was a trick of the light, a classic auctioneer's ploy. The stamps were the stamps, but you were tempted to pay more because of how you were made to perceive them. Value shone from their surface until they attained the appearance of priceless art.

'So, you're a freelance journalist with an interest in stamps,' Richard Watkins told me when I first sat opposite him at his desk. He went on, 'That's a dangerous combination.'

Watkins was fifty-seven, and had been in the stamp business for thirty years, including a lengthy period at Stanley Gibbons. He told me that he gave Mark Brandon his first job. He said he was suspicious of journalists because no matter how clearly he tried to explain something, they always got an important detail wrong, and he sometimes ended up looking foolish. A recent example was the George V Prussian Blue, an error of colour printed in 1935. George V had approved a $2^{1}/2$d stamp in ultramarine, but four sheets were inadvertently printed in a far richer turquoise. The stamps sell for more than £10,000 each, and every time one of them reaches a record price at auction, Watkins gets phone calls. 'About five hundred of them, and everyone thinks they've got the rare colour, a stamp worth a fortune rather than just a few pounds.' He said he feels like hiding under his desk when the calls start coming in.

Watkins's office was upstairs, his room packed with auction catalogues from the past. As ever, the early ones were heartbreaking: a mint block of 1840 Twopenny Blues for a couple of thousand pounds. Before I discussed the possible sale of my stamps, I told him I was most interested in what will happen to stamp collecting in fifty years' time, with so few young people coming through.

'Of course, none of us actually really knows,' he said. 'Sadly, as each generation passes the interest is less and less. But it ain't going to disappear, I can tell you that. There seems to be a lot of interest in researching family history and genealogy, and I think that will lead to more of an interest in stamps. And in the upper echelons I think it will remain extremely serious and be very keenly followed.'

He said there was a distinction to be drawn between the UK and the rest of the world. 'In Europe it's always been a well-respected pastime, whereas in the UK it has always been the shoddy mac brigade. The problem is, in the UK the items are getting so expensive. They are realising their true value, but soon it will move into the echelons where just the basic items will cost £10,000, £15,000, £20,000. It's becoming a little bit more like the art world.'

As Watson spoke I thought suddenly of Maria Sharapova. The Russian tennis player was nineteen, and when she appeared at Wimbledon as a former champion in 2006 she was asked what she did when she wasn't on the circuit. She liked to collect stamps, she said, and the press room perked up. In most interviews these young players said that they liked to hang out at the mall and be just like other teenagers, and everyone yawned because (a) they would *never* be just like other teenagers, and (b) if they ever went to the mall it was usually by special arrangement, at a time when other teenagers were not admitted. But now Sharapova was doing something that famous teenagers hardly ever did, go to the post office to buy commemoratives.

'I've collected stamps since I was nine or ten years old,' she said. How many did she have? 'I've so many, millions. I've stamps passed down from my mum's grandmother. They're that old they're almost rusty! The coolest thing is finding an excuse to go to the post office and do something different. It's exciting. Not too many people do it. It's a cool collection I have. I know the whole process of how to remove stamps and dry them, but now I get catalogues from around the world and I get my mum to order them. I look at them and enjoy them. It's a nice distraction away from tennis.'

Sharapova was clearly a freak, but her enthusiasm was encouraging. Richard Watkins said there weren't many like her in his auction rooms. In fact, there were very few collectors under fifty. Certainly this was true of the auction Spink had held at the big Washington convention – mostly elderly men with shiny temples.

'I've heard a lot of theories as to why people collect,' Watkins continued, 'and the most popular one now is that collectors have to own, they have to gather, they have to have this stuff. Someone associated it with an unhappy childhood. If you felt unloved as a child you could at least get these items together and love them and cherish them.'

I told him that I had a very loved childhood.

'Well, I did. I have an interest in diecast aircraft. They're worth quite a few quid, some of them. They're toys really. But I have a space problem. And I collect postcards and postal history from Barnet, Whetstone, Potters Bar and Welwyn.'

Watkins had collected stamps since he was twelve, and a year later he was working part-time in a stamp shop. 'If I won the lottery I'd be an absolute mug for Empire stamps of Victoria, with a specialisation in certain areas. Once it's in you it's in you. I know people who would starve for a week in order to buy a stamp. Or people who, every time I see them, they're still wearing the same pair of trousers and shirt. And try selling a catalogue subscription to those people – collectors don't want a catalogue subscription, they want to spend all their money on stamps.'

I then produced my album of errors, and I think he was fairly impressed. 'Mmm,' he said, 'there's some nice things here.' He turned the page, 'Yes, very nice.' At the end, he said, 'There's no question, it's better than I had expected. Some very nice things.' But should I sell to Spink or to a dealer, specifically Brandon?

'If you know what's it worth and what you paid for it and what you want for it, then you could certainly sell it lock, stock and barrel. Dealers can pay good prices. Of course, we'd love to have it, but I can't guarantee what you'll get for it at auction. We do very well with errors, but it's not our ultimate strength. But in an auction you have to make it interesting for people. You can't put the reserve price on too high, because you won't sell it, it will put people off. If you sell it to a dealer and you're happy with the offer, you may very well have got more at auction but you'll never know.' Earlier he had told me, 'Brandon knows what he's doing.'

As Watkins looked through the album, I said that on my way here I felt slightly heartbroken to be selling them at all. 'It happens,' Watkins said. 'I'm like a surgeon most of the time. I'm dealing with people who have been collecting for sixty years sometimes, and it's like cutting their arms off. They just don't want to let them go. But you know, the Three Ds.'

Here they came again.

'Divorce, debt and death.'

Before I had gone to Spink, I had taken the album to my marriage guidance counsellor.

My marriage had stalled long before my affair. We didn't row, we didn't throw things at each other – perhaps that was the problem. We stopped communicating emotionally. We ran out of projects.

We were married in August 1987, we had our first child

within a year, our second two years later. We were reliant on each other for different things, solving problems as we went, finding new projects – first our love, then our house, then bringing up our children – until we ran out of projects and the problem became ourselves. For a long while our two boys became the great and loved ambition in our lives, and when they grew increasingly independent in their mid-teens I began to look around for new things – new ways to tell stories in my work, new ways to spend my earnings, new obsessions. My wife was the same. Her work went in new directions. My interests were mostly practical, hers increasingly spiritual. She was not interested in used postage.

My new girlfriend was never a great one for stamps either – I'm not sure that I could ever be attracted to any woman who was. But she was one for letters, and I treasure her writing. I never corresponded much with my wife; we were together all the time, so what was the point? In the last few years, we weren't very romantic like that, which is such a cause of sadness. But girlfriends are something else, and my affair has produced so much passion on so much paper. The stamps remain on the envelopes.

We had come to marriage guidance not to save our marriage but to save our souls. We wanted to understand what had happened and do our best for our children and our future. There was a bit of shouting during the sessions, and some crying, but we made good progress. In fact, I felt that everything was going smoothly until the marriage guidance counsellor had done such a good job in delving into my past that I became convinced that I had gone out with her when I was about ten. One classic requirement for successful therapy is that the therapist must remain a blank canvas. This means that you don't find out anything about the person you're paying £50 to each week. I once asked her, at the end of a particularly traumatic session, where she was going on her holiday, and she explained why she wasn't keen to tell me. Or she would tell me, but it wasn't generally done. I might think, perhaps, that if she said the Maldives she was charging me too much for the sessions.

She said Italy and Portugal.

So I certainly wasn't allowed to ask about her marital status or her marital happiness, or her age, or whether or not she had children, or whether she had ever had an affair, or how she had dealt with desire. Fair enough. But then I began to wonder whether Jenny – that was her name – her real name, I was sure, was the Jenny who was also my first-ever girlfriend, the strict Catholic girl from Gospel Oak whom I had spent many weekends with wearing a maroon velvet jacket and thinking I was It.

When I told Jenny of my intention to sell my errors, she did what she invariably did best in these situations: delved for deeper meaning. She made the connection between my stamps and my missing family, and she saw that their sale (the selling of my mistakes) might signify a new start for me. But what were my own errors? I did not consider the affair that broke up my marriage to be a mistake, although I regret the terrible hurt and upheaval it caused. I fell in love and I felt helpless, whisked away from normal life to blissful insanity. Occasionally I thought that my greatest error had been revealing the affair to my wife in the first place. But I hated the continual lies, and I couldn't have lived with myself.

At least there were no further romantic revelations at marriage guidance. On further questioning it turned out that Jenny was not my long-lost first love, to which the only response I could offer was 'phew'.

*

Brandon took me to lunch in Linda's soft-top Merc. I asked how they had met, and he said that he was in Sotheby's one day doing some viewing, and Linda, then an exchange student, also happened to be looking around, and it went from there. Brandon, who was divorced, said that he and Linda might get married soon, 'for tax reasons'. I told him that after years of living together my wife and I got married for tax reasons too. 'It's the best reason,' Brandon said.

Over our meal he said that he still gets the same buzz from stamps that he always did. 'The price is secondary for me – the first thing I say when I look at a nice item is, "Oh, isn't that gorgeous . . . a rare postmark . . . a special block."'

The Blue Mauritius came up in our conversation, and he sighed, as if recalling a former lover. 'Ah, one of the aristocrats of philately . . . Seeing one of those as a small boy would be like seeing God.' I remembered seeing one myself as a small boy, albeit in a Billy Bunter book. But now I wasn't rooting for Bunter any more, but for the cad Sir Hilton Popper.

Brandon said that following the death of Sir Gawaine Baillie, his main client was Russian. We talked about other things I might collect if I stopped collecting errors. Sea Horses, I thought, but he said, 'Sea Horses can be incredibly expensive these days. I still reckon you should try British North America, New Brunswick, Nova Scotia, beautiful stamps. If I was an investor with £100,000 I'd rather put it in early BNA than I would in early GB. There's more potential. You look at a Penny Black, a nice one will cost you £200. But a Threepenny Beaver of Canada, ten, no twenty times rarer, will cost you less than £200. But you like GB, so . . . I can sort you out with a nice high-value collection of a lot of things. I can sort you out with a nice £5 orange for £4,000. Used. With a certificate.'

I asked him about the best error he had ever found. He didn't think long. Twenty years ago he bought a rubbish collection for a few pounds, including a lot of Penny Reds in an old tobacco tin. His son had only just started taking an interest in stamps. 'They were in my office, and one evening I was going to go to bed, and Mark said, "Can I go through all those stamps?"

'So I go upstairs, have a bath, and I'm lying on my bed when there's a knock on the door.

'He says, "Dad, I've found a Penny Red with no lettering in one corner."'

Theoretically this was the 'B-blank, Plate 77', a famously rare error.

'I thought, "No, he's having me on." But then I realised, "Hang on, he wouldn't know about that . . ."

'So I got out of bed and said, "Show it to me."

'And sure enough he had found a B-blank, which in those days was worth £3,000–£4,000. In a rubbish tin of nothing. I wouldn't have even opened the tin. I would have just sold it on for a few pounds. So they are out there. I sold one recently to another dealer for £13,500. I bet today if I had a tin of Penny Reds Mark wouldn't even look, but in those days he was keen.'

After lunch I sold him my stamps.

He wrote me a cheque for £42,500. We haggled over the last £500, and when he agreed in his actorly way to pay it ('Oh all right then, but I'll hardly be able to eat next week') I knew that he had done remarkably well out of the deal. But I had got back what I paid for them and a little more – I had done particularly well out of the missing Post Office Towers, bought for £2,000, sold for twice that – and I could now afford to pay mortgages, credit card bills, maintenance and university fees. I might even be able to buy a new car.

I was already beginning to miss my stamps when I drove

home with Brandon's cheque. I thought about how much larger the cheque could have been had I hung on to them for five years more. But I needed the money now, because of another unreasoning passion in my life.

I felt a little cleaner as I arrived back at my rented flat. I no longer had secrets or something to hide away in a cupboard. But I also no longer had my beautiful, delicate, irreplaceable stamps.

I was in the front of the queue at the bank with my paying-in book the following morning. The bank clerk asked me if I had plans for the money, and would I like to speak to an adviser. 'Oh no,' I said. 'It's not for me, it's for my divorce.'

I didn't sell absolutely everything. I sold all my expensive items, all my great errors. But I kept my core collection of GB from 1953 to 2006, the normal stamps without imperfection that are worth about £2,500 in total. I kept my box of oddments – first-day covers, presentation packs, blocks of fours from various issues – worth about £300. I kept my earliest Gay Venture album with my glued-in stamps, worth less than £1. And I kept four first-day covers from Heinz, all with animals, to remind me of our trip to the zoo.

And I had some cheap fakes. These were famous stamps in their own right – the so-called Maryland Forgeries of which very little is known except for the American state in which they were printed. These consisted of all the famous GB missing colour errors – the Tower, the missing Minis, the Red Cross missing red – but they wouldn't have fooled a ten year old. The perforations were too stubby, the colour was weak, the paper felt thin and looked far too white. Also, they cost about £3 each from a respectable dealer, who sold them as a novelty item with 'forgery' printed on the back.

The day after I sold my stamps I spoke to Melanie Kilim

again about her unusual fear of the Post Office Tower. Then I walked to the postbox at the end of my road and sent her a Maryland Forgery of the Tower stamp with the missing olive-green. I hoped that, for the first time in her life, she would enjoy the stamp without reservations. In fact, the opposite occurred. She wanted to know the answer to a question that, more calmly expressed, might have been a Zen riddle: if the tower wasn't on the stamp, 'Then where the hell was it?' She said that the stamp gave her palpitations.

I was tempted to reply, 'I know exactly what you mean.'

Postscript

I thought my relationship with David Brandon would end with stamps. But then it spilled over into cars.

I had once spent a very arduous lunchtime talking to a computer engineer about his modern $QE2$ errors, and after an hour of nothing he said one very interesting thing. He had bought many of his stamps from Brandon, and described him as 'almost a father figure'. I knew what he meant by this. Brandon was paternal in a number of ways, and ideally so. He was friendly, generous, fine at his job, older, he cared for his sons, he was knowledgeable and full of guidance.

Apart from stamps, Brandon spent his money on cars. The only other man I had met who had a private car collection – i.e. cars that would never be seen picking up from schools or buying food – was Nick Freeman, the lawyer known as Mr Loophole for his skill in getting David Beckham and Alex Ferguson out of the clutches of the traffic police. Freeman opened up his Knutsford garage and showed me his Bentley and his BMW. Brandon opened up his garage one day to show me his Jaguar, his Porsche Turbo, Linda's soft-top Mercedes. The Jaguar, which had thirty thousand miles on it ('barely run in!') had every conceivable gadget and luxury, and the most beautiful stitching on the leather. The cars' number plates were DB-something, just as Freeman's were NF-something.

A few weeks after I had sold him my stamps, I returned to Guildford to see Brandon about another Jaguar he wanted to show me. I sat in his office as he found the keys, and his girlfriend Linda came in wearing a very short skirt.

'Would you like a sandwich?' she asked.

'I would.'

'A salmon sandwich?'

'A salmon sandwich would be good, and some tea even better.'

'Not too much salmon please, Linda,' David said. 'Don't overload it.'

He said that the Jaguar he was about to show me was simply staggering. Brandon had previously sent me a couple of emails about the car. He had bought it from a nearby dealer, a friend of his, and he thought it represented an absolute bargain. It cost £4,000, which, considering I had almost bought a stamp from him at that price, seemed to be quite good value. Brandon confirmed this by saying 'it's an awful lot of car'. He had bought the car for his son Mark, but Mark had decided he didn't need it, living in Portugal and all that with a Range Rover and a Porsche Cayenne. David had bought it for Mark to run around Guildford in when he came to visit, but it was always easier just to hire a car at the airport for a few days. So it was now on the market, and I was in the garage first in line. Brandon emailed that I would be the car's third owner. New it would have cost about £50,000 fully spec'd. I replied that I was certainly happy to take it for a test drive around his private roads. In one email Brandon said that he hoped it wouldn't be raining when I came down, as that would be such a shame on the polish.

*

In his office I told him that I found it impossible to see myself in his big car. 'How old is Mark?' I asked.

'Thirty-seven, I think.'

'I'm forty-six, but I still feel too young for a Jag. Is that a terrible thing to say?'

'It's a ridiculous thing to say. I had a Jaguar when I was twenty-one. No, I think I was younger. It was an E-Type, I hasten to add.'

We talked about types, about the E-Type, the S-Types and the X-Types.

'The S-Types are a little bit ugly,' Brandon said, 'but the X-Types are quite pretty, I think. In fact, I saw one the other day that was an absolute cracker. I actually went to look at it. It was 2002, three-litre, four-wheel drive with everything on – everything apart from sat-nav, which you can plug in so it's not a problem – blue with cream hide or parchment I think they call it, twenty-five thousand miles, so nicely run-in. Twelve grand! Unbelievable!'

Brandon walked me to the garage. This wasn't his main garage with his posh cars, but another one a few hundred feet away. As he unlocked the door, he explained that he was about to show me a very special thing, a vehicle that was almost in exactly the same condition as it was when it rolled off the production line twelve years earlier. The Jag was a deep red – not the racing green I would have preferred – and it had done seventy-five thousand miles ('nicely run in'). Brandon revealed the car by removing a large white sheet that was keeping it from unwanted dust and damp. It was a gesture not unfamiliar to fans of the Norwich-based quiz show *Sale of the Century*, the big reveal of the big prize at the end of every episode. Brandon's car was indeed immaculate and carefully polished, and had every conceivable luxury apart from sat-nav. The display panel lit up like

Kyoto at night, and anything you needed to know was there in dancing LED – which, when the model first appeared in the mid-1980s, represented the very epitome of bachelor style. It was a Sovereign XJ140, and it reminded me of the sort of cars my parents' male friends would drive to their boardrooms. Once, at the age of about eleven, I got a lift back from a Tottenham v. Chelsea match from a man called Henry in a Jaguar or a Daimler, and I felt a little bit lost in the back of it, sliding around on the leather. At that moment I knew two things: that the car Henry was driving was very expensive, and that I would never own one. It wasn't the sort of car I wanted or liked. It was too flat, too plush, too effortless, too boring. It was obviously an old man's car. And now here I was, being schmoozed into one, and thinking positively about it.

I was tempted, but I had qualms. The car was over-immaculate. It wouldn't play well in the London streets overnight. Some knobhead would key it, or the city rain would make it look dirty every other day. Or it would get dented, which I wouldn't actually mind myself, but I feared people would take pity on me. Also, it seemed like a big car to manoeuvre and park, and it was obviously a guzzler, perhaps 18 m.p.g.

Another problem was that I had only recently bought another old car, an iridium blue Saab 900 H reg from 1990, the same model and colour Saab I had bought when my second son was born and which had served us well until my wife was at the wheel in 1999 and a milk float reversed into it and the insurers wrote it off. This had done ninety-two thousand miles and would cost a lot in repairs, but it was a classic, and I couldn't resist it, not because it reminded me of my younger self, but because it was a very cool object with a low chassis and long nose and was a pleasure to drive after a decade of automatic things from Japan. I would have to sell the Saab if

I bought the Jag, and would probably make a loss on it, just like I had feared I would do on my stamps.

But the final problem with the Jag was the fact that it was an old man's car. I said to Brandon, 'I'm not sure anyone under sixty who isn't on the board of directors at some small manufacturing company with their own reserved parking space could comfortably drive one of these things.'

Brandon said: 'Nonsense!'

A few weeks later I came down to look at the Jaguar for a second time. I had studied the magazines, including *Practical Classics*, which had lots of tips on restoring wheel trims and checking for oil leaks. I had also told my new lover about it, and she said I should keep the Saab because the Jag was an old man's car.

There was indeed something great about those classic Saabs, the 99s and the 900s, before General Motors took over and ruined them. Now it was impossible to buy a new Saab with a hatch:* one of the key things that defined it and made first-time drivers into loyal fans. My first experience of a Saab was having a lift away from the *Independent on Sunday* one day with Sebastian Faulks, when he was still the literary editor and before he hit the jackpot with *Birdsong*. Faulks had a turbo model, which suffered famously from turbo lag. He showed me what this meant as we sped up City Road one evening. He put his foot down and drew breath. Nothing. Then someone appeared to strap a rocket to the exhaust and off we hurtled. Faulks grinned, and I had the feeling I wasn't the first to be entertained in this way. Saabs have always had literary connections in London. Ian McEwan drove an old one, and Julian Barnes had been loyal to the brand for years. Even the people who sold them were full of stories. A dealer in Finchley called

* Unless you bought an ugly Estate.

Neil Franklin, whose dad played the vibes, once told me about The Who at the Isle of Wight festival. The band was on after Hendrix, and Pete Townshend was in his wasted phase. Hendrix blew his mind, the force of his performance so over-whelming that when The Who took the stage Townshend couldn't even tune his guitar properly. He threw his Gibson across the stage, and that guitar eventually found its way to the home of my Saab dealer. Apparently.

I bought my first Saab within a couple of weeks of that ride with Faulks, a standard model not a turbo. It was a great car, but after a while I just took it for granted. I didn't join any owners' clubs or attend rallies, and I didn't have many Saab conversations. But one day not long after I had begun writing about the fall and rise of British wrestling I went down to Kent to see Jackie Pallo. Max Crabtree, brother of Big Daddy Shirley Crabtree, had told me that Jackie Pallo used to be one of the all-time greats, and as proof of this he alerted me to the fact that 'he changed his Saab every year'. I had heard about these sorts of people, although I only tended to mix with those who hung on to their cars until they exploded. Jackie Pallo and his son Jackie Pallo Jnr were initially a bit suspicious of me, the way all old wrestlers are when they meet a journalist. These days everyone knows wrestling was a real sport, but back then there was a widespread belief that it was all fixed. The wrestlers liked to wait until reporters had asked them whether it was all choreographed, and then apply a headlock so painful that the journalist thought they were going to die.

I arrived at Pallo's house on a sweltering summer's day, and he picked me up at Ramsgate station in his Saab, and I told him that I drove the same model. 'Simon,' he said in a measured tone, 'I have lots of Saabs.' This turned out to be true. Pallo collected Saabs. There were eight or nine of them parked on the overgrown verge by his house, each with a different level of rust. He used to drive hundreds of thousands of miles to his fights in these cars, and now he couldn't bear to part with them. When Jackie Jr came out of the house to join us in the garden, his father immediately put his mind at rest as to my trustworthiness. 'It's all right,' he explained as he put his arm around my shoulder. 'He's a Saab man.'

A decade later, I wondered what becoming a Jag man might entail. What would it say about me, other than that I was still clearly susceptible to Brandon's sales patter and had an eye for a bargain? But what if it wasn't a bargain? What if it was another error? I knew very little about cars, and, like most Jewish men, I began to feel uneasy when the bonnet was unlatched. I could barely manage an oil change. There were certain things I knew to look out for. A strange engine noise. Rust. Bubbling chrome. But beyond that there were unprecedented possibilities of mechanical badness. I was thinking of calling in one of those RAC guys who give the car the once-over and then give you the nod or the shake, but I felt nervous of doing this in Brandon's presence. It seemed like an insult, as if I didn't trust him to buy a nice car for his son.

'Pete,' Brandon said to his other son, 'you can bring the car round anytime now.' Brandon told me that the car was now out of MOT and tax, and came without any sort of warranty. 'If the door drops off tomorrow there isn't a lot you can do about it apart from buy a new door.' As we waited for the car to appear, Brandon told me that he'd been buying so much material that he really didn't know when he was going to catalogue it all – he reckoned he was about eighteen months behind. He just had too much expertising to do – he thought he dispensed about three thousand certificates a year. He also said he'd just come back from a weekend in Monaco with Linda, at which he'd spent almost 800,000 euros at one auction.*

The car arrived out front. 'Look at this chrome,' Brandon purred. 'They just don't do this any more. We climbed inside and I found the button that glided back the seat. 'The back seat is virtually unused in twelve years,' Brandon said. 'The front seats are heated . . . two owners . . .' He pulled out the cigarette lighter and looked at it. 'Not even a smoker!' Brandon told me he had recently driven the car down to Andover, and it purred all the way. Not driving it was a sin, he reasoned, a real crime locking it up in a garage all the time. I was beginning to feel sorry for a shank of metal. We prowled around his estate and into the driveway of the Vice-Chancellor of Surrey University who lived near by. It was a stately parade, and I drove slowly enough to examine the cruise control and hi-fi, and I started to feel like my dad.

My father never had a Jag, but I imagined that if he didn't aspire to a Sovereign he probably longed for an E-Type. He certainly could have afforded one, but perhaps he felt it was a car without irony, a car that didn't say anything about its driver other than 'I've bought a Jag!'. But now a man in his mid-forties driving a red 1994 model meant something else, something more complex. If it didn't mean I had style, perhaps it meant I was an individualist. I had something most other people at my age didn't, which is a state of affairs I'd always

---

* He could afford to. Within a few days of selling Brandon my stamps, they were on his website at twice the price. I had expected this. I had once seen him bid at an auction for a unique British error (the 1964 6d Botanical Conference with yellow flowers omitted), landing it for under £20,000. A week later, you could buy it on his website stamperrors.com for £42,500, the exact price I had got from Brandon for my entire collection. A week after that it was still there, but now the cost was 'Price on Request'.

longed for. And I was taking a risk – about how I'd be perceived, about whether I owned something that would last. I wondered what my dad would have thought about me driving around those private roads. Would he have felt pride? Would he have acknowledged a yearning that would never be fulfilled? Would he have liked the colour?

And when I thought about my father I also wondered what he would have made of my adventures with stamps. Perhaps in time he would have appreciated my lifelong interest, and seen them as more than postage. He would have seen their value rise, and observed what could be learnt about the world from philately. I considered whether he would have got on with Brandon, and I imagined he would; they both liked order and efficiency, and they delighted in a sense of propriety.

I also thought about how my life had become entwined with postal life. My brother had worked at the Royal Free Hospital, and both my children were born there – its outer wall bears a Blue Plaque proclaiming that Rowland Hill lived here in his latter years until his death in 1879; for half of my life I walked through Rowland Hill Street on my way to Belsize Park Tube station. More recently, I have lived in a house in St Ives, Cornwall, called the Old Post Office Garage, a converted building that once sheltered Royal Mail delivery vans and still has a GPO wicker basket under the stairs where we keep beach gear.

And there was another Rowland Hill address that came to mean something unexpected. In January 2007 I received an email from a man called John Fulljames, the Artistic Director of The Opera Group. He was directing a new opera called *The Shops* for a touring production later in the year, the highlight of which was a few days at the Linbury Theatre, the studio theatre of the Royal Opera House. He had read a piece I had written about my love of stamps, and wondered whether I would write the programme notes for the opera, anything on the theme of collecting, obsession and consumerism, the big themes of *The Shops*. I said I would, especially if I could attend rehearsals and come to a performance. I wrote the piece, and in early July made my way to the Jerwood Space rehearsal room in Southwark. From Southwark Tube station I passed the Rowland Hill estate, but there was a better surprise when I arrived.

'You know you're in it?' John Fulljames told me.

'In what?'

'Obliquely, you're in the opera. Your name.'

I had read the libretto before I wrote my programme notes, but I must have read it at speed. In the rehearsals they ran through the following passage, sung by a police officer called Oliver to a judge (the policeman is reading out a list of stamps allegedly stolen by the opera's anti-hero).

Oliver: The Belk Medal, eighty, phosphor-treated paper. Distant Galaxies, twenty, *tête-bêche* pair. Two Hundred and Fiftieth Anniversary of the Death of La Bruyère, commemorative stamp, retouched. The Garfield Tower, forty, embossed printing, single copy. The Postal Service in Greenland, Then and Now, fifteen, thirty, fifty, steel plate engraving, watermark.

Never mind the Postal Service in Greenland, my name was finally on a stamp, albeit a fictional one. John Fulljames told me it was a direct reference to my love of the Post Office Tower error, and I was overwhelmed with gratitude. In fact, I was still blushing when I left the rehearsal room. *The Garfield Tower, forty, embossed printing, single copy.* And then I thought, 'Imagine *singing* that . . .'

Before I made a decision on the car, Brandon took me for lunch again at the Squires Holt. It was getting on for Christmas, and every table was decked with crackers and booked for parties. But Brandon came here often – in fact, it was the third time we had been in together – and a table was made up especially for him, the way they used to do for Sammy Davis Jr in Las Vegas clubs.

We talked a little about his divorce. I told him that my own divorce proceedings are under way and that it's been an amicable split, a credit to our marriage guidance counsellor. We talk about my children, seventeen and nineteen as I turn forty-eight, and how well they have handled the split, and how much I love them, and how glad I am that we are still very close. And how they still believed stamp collecting to be a hobby of enduring sadness. My affair had broken up after fourteen months and I was now with someone new. I think of this whole period as the most exciting time of my life, as well as the most damaging.

On the way in Linda's Merc he had told me about something very special he wanted to show me when we got back to his house. He made me promise that he would only show it to me on the understanding that officially I hadn't seen it. I couldn't eat my Christmas pudding fast enough.

When we got back, I sat in his office while he went to another room. I heard him clicking the wheels on the safe. 'Now you remember what we said,' he said.

'That I hadn't seen it.'

'Exactly. As far as you're concerned, this doesn't exist.'

Then he produced a small brown envelope with a stiffened back, and took from it a transparent sheath. Inside the envelope was one of the rarest and most famous philatelic items in the world. It was unique. Its whereabouts had been unknown for about a quarter of a century, and here it was on the outskirts of Guildford. He took down from his shelf a couple of hardback books describing the item; each devoted an entire page to its photograph. 'I've already sold it on,' he told me. 'I'll be delivering it by hand next week.'

I had a close look at it, and I felt privileged to hold it. It had an aura. I had met famous film stars who had a similar glow. It was a worldwide philatelic object of lust. I felt sure that even people who weren't that keen on stamps would be entranced by it. It was a perfect specimen, something far greater in one's own hands than one could possibly detect from even the best reproductions. I asked Brandon whether he would be sad to part with it.

'Not really, he said. 'It has been a childhood dream just to see it, and to have owned it for a while is a dream come true. To be honest, it will be a relief. It is worth much much more than this house. In forty years it is by far the most expensive item I have ever handled, by a huge margin.'

I didn't buy the car.

The 1966 GB stamp with the missing Jaguar cost £8,000, and the real thing with leather and heated seats cost half that. But the fuel consumption would have been ridiculous, and then there was the parking, the risk, the absurdity of my driving a gentleman's slab like that . . . but mostly I didn't buy it because I had convinced myself I didn't need it, an adult purchasing decision that had never really bothered me before. The car didn't have a scratch on it, but that didn't make it desirable. Obviously, I had always liked wrecked beauty and spoilt, fragile things. I had been offered something that may be without error, apart from the error of my buying it in the first place.

And when I drove back in my Saab, my neck stiffening with every gear change, I wondered whether I would ever see Brandon again. I had finished with the car business. I had no need to buy stamps from him in the future. But over lunch, with most of my errors in his safe, we had talked about the possibility of building a nice little British Victorian collection, starting at the beginning with the Penny Black and the Twopenny Blue, and going all the way through the reign. It would be an expensive endeavour, but a rewarding one. I'd learn a lot of history, and I'd value the quest.

'You would need some guidance,' Brandon said to me, 'but it could be a good investment.'

I told him I'd think about it. And the more I thought about it, the more it seemed like a wonderful idea.

Acknowledgements

Thank you to everyone who helped me with this book. I am particularly grateful to Ian Jack for commissioning the story for *Granta* that got this whole thing moving. I would also like to thank all those who gave up their time to talk to me about my family, about collecting, and about stamps.

As always, Julian Loose at Faber and Pat Kavanagh have been my most faithful supporters.

And finally to Ben, Jake, Diane, Annie and Justine, who saw me through.